THE POWER OF THE BLACK VOTE AND GOVERNMENT TACTICS TO BLOCK IT

THE POWER OF THE BLACK VOTE AND GOVERNMENT TACTICS TO BLOCK IT

JOJO VARLACK-HICKS

NEW DEGREE PRESS

COPYRIGHT © 2020 JOJO VARLACK-HICKS

THE POWER OF THE BLACK VOTE

AND GOVERNMENT TACTICS TO BLOCK IT

ISBN   978-1-63676-578-5   *Paperback*

      978-1-63676-191-6   *Kindle Ebook*

      978-1-63676-194-7   *Ebook*

The vote is precious. It's almost sacred, so go out and vote like you never voted before.

JOHN LEWIS

TABLE OF CONTENTS

———

FOREWORD

In this timely, provocative book, JoJo Varlack-Hicks clearly and thought-provokingly addresses the efforts made by those in power to continue their quest to deprive blacks of their constitutional right to vote. She also challenges the blacks at who the oppressors' efforts are directed to cease from aiding the oppressors by failing to exercise their right to vote and failing to encourage other blacks to vote.

JoJo brings to this writing the passion, critical thinking, and discernment she exhibited in her studies as a student at Fort Valley State University. I enjoyed reading this outstanding book just as much as I enjoyed reading her essays and other writings as her major professor.

This is a book that is certain to educate, motivate, and energize the apathetic black citizen to exercise his constitutional right to vote, and encourage those fighting to secure that right to continue the fight!

Gregory Homer

THE POWER OF THE BLACK VOTE: A CLARION CALL TO ACTION

I have known JoJo for thirty years and trust her wisdom and prescient judgments. Her book clearly establishes the case against systemic voter suppression designed to disenfranchise voters of color and maintain white political power. JoJo began writing this timely book more than a year ago—prior to the most recent, blatant, and almost daily acts of voter suppression designed to bypass the people's will and reelect Donald Trump as president.

The Power of the Black Vote should be read by all Americans, regardless of ethnicity, color, or religious persuasion, because if successful, in this age of precise electronic targeting of voters, these tactics can be deployed against any segment of voters opposed to the agenda of those in power regardless of race, color, previous condition of servitude, sex, or age. Moreover, those employing these suppression tactics will never have to cede power. At this point, voting will become a perfunctory endorsement of whichever political cabal has succeeded in wresting the power of the ballot from the people.

Abraham Lincoln reportedly described the ballot as being stronger than a bullet in an 1856 address to the Republican State Convention. His election by the people four years later came on the precipice of a war that threatened the unity of our nation. It was the power of the ballot that positioned Lincoln, with a single-minded will, to preserve the Union. In doing so, he emancipated a formerly enslaved people and set in motion a series of amendments and laws leading to their equal treatment under the law and ultimately the Voting Rights Act, by which they were granted the power of the ballot to preserve their hard-won rights.

The quote attributed to Lincoln likely came from an August 26, 1863, letter to longtime friend, James C. Conkling, in which he wrote, "To be quite plain you are dissatisfied with me about the negro [sic]. Quite likely there is a difference of opinion between you and myself [sic] on this subject. . . . You dislike the emancipation proclamation; and, perhaps would have it retracted. . . . [T]here can be no successful appeal from the ballot to the bullet; and that [sic] they who take such an appeal are sure to lose their case and pay the cost."

Ironically, in an act that is the ultimate goal of voter dis-enfranchisement and suppression, voters were denied the voice of their vote when a little more than two years later and a short five months following his reelection, Lincoln was assassinated on April 15, 1865. What eventually followed was a period of robust black political participation, including election to public office, and then the slow unwinding of the hard-won political gains. As JoJo asserts, the fear of this power was unleashed and a resulting loss of white power as America became increasingly brown is now fueling recent voter suppression activities.

The right to vote is a fundamental constitutional right that cannot be abridged or denied by the federal or state governments on account of race, color, or previous condition servitude, sex, or age (Fifteenth, Nineteenth, and Twenty-Sixth Constitutional Amendments).

Despite these protections, recent and blatant attacks on the right to vote threaten the very foundation of our Constitution and democracy:

- Federal – Removal of mailboxes and mail sorting equipment, and reduction of overtime and service hours by the postal service threatens to delay the counting of mail-in ballots.
- Florida – In an effort to subvert the votes of 1.5 million formerly incarcerated persons, Florida's governor and its Republican legislature added to the law restoring voter rights what amounts to a poll tax, by requiring those whose voting rights were restored to pay all fines and fees from their sentence before they are permitted to vote. Florida was a must-win state in President Trump's re-election bid.
- Illinois – Black voters were targeted in a robocall attempting to dissuade them from mailing in their ballots with

misinformation indicating their personal information would be added to a public database and they could face arrest for outstanding warrants or be forced to participate in COVID-19 vaccine trials.

- Texas – Governor Greg Abbott removed mail-in ballot drop boxes and ordered the return of ballots to a single clerk's office in every county, further limiting a voter's ability to participate in the 2020 election on the pretext of preventing unproven voter fraud.
- Federal – The president of the United States sought to intimidate voters by calling on "his" supporters to "watch" the polls.

However, protection of the ballot is only one step in the process of preserving our democracy as we again find ourselves on the precipice of a great war. We must respond by electing politicians who will take a hard stance on homegrown terrorists and militia—which Trump has refused to do—that again threaten to take by the bullet that which they cannot win with the ballot.

Every American who loves their democratic freedoms should read this book, which is written in an easily understood manner and accessible to all, and heed its warning.

Carolyn Quick Tillery, Esquire

Author, *The African-American Heritage Cookbook* Series

INTRODUCTION

If you don't know what happened behind you, you won't know what is happening in front of you.[1]

JOE MADISON

As a child growing up in Georgia in the 1960s, I had this question in my head: "Why do they (white people) hate us so much?" I remember watching television and seeing the teeth of German shepherds deeply gripped onto the legs of black men; water shooting from the hoses of fire hydrants so forcefully that black men and women were knocked to the ground; and policemen, the very people who were supposed to protect us, were doing nothing of the sort, but instead were beating black men with billy clubs and dragging bloody bodies off like trash. I remember looking at the news coverage of President John F. Kennedy being shot, crying uncontrollably, and asking myself, "Why, Lord?" This scenario repeated itself when his brother Robert Kennedy and Dr. Martin Luther

---

[1] Joe Madison, SiriusXM, *Urban View*, Channel 126, accessed 2015.

King, Jr. were also killed. Each died fighting for the equality of all mankind. Those were challenging times in our country.

Why were black men and women treated with such cruelty? Simple. They wanted to exercise their constitutional right to vote—a right under a few amendments in the United States Constitution:

1. Amendment Fourteen, ratified July 9, 1868, Citizenship Rights, Equal Protection, Apportionment, Civil War Debt (weren't black people citizens?); and
2. Amendment Fifteen, ratified February 3, 1870, Right to Vote Not Denied by Race (doesn't this include black men?).[2]

If these amendments included black men, why did our government come up with so many illegal tactics to prevent blacks from voting? Furthermore, why to this day does our government continue coming up with tactics to prevent not just the black vote, but the votes of many minority citizens whose skin color is not white?

Years passed after the Civil Rights Act of 1964. While things appeared to get better, the more they changed, the more they stayed the same. The spoken and unspoken rules for blacks were much different than those for whites. Before I continue, it is important to explain the use of the terms "blacks" and "whites." In the early 1960s, these were the predominant races. Changes in the laws were based on the unfair treatment of

---

2   National Constitution Center, "Fourteenth and Fifteenth Amendments," accessed April 3, 2020.

blacks. Allow me to further say that when I speak of white people, I cannot and will not clump all whites as perpetrators, for many whites stood and died alongside blacks for the rights to vote and to fair treatment, just as they are today! Lastly, much of what is discussed is uncomfortable yet necessary. Like anything in life, when issues are not addressed, they fester and eventually rupture. America has ruptured and now the issues must be discussed if we are to get past this. We cannot continue avoiding the elephant in the room because it is very obvious.

HOW I BECAME INTERESTED IN VOTING RIGHTS

I attended Georgetown University and studied Policy Leadership. The first class on policymaking was very interesting and encouraged me to learn more. In the second class, though, I was bored stiff, not because of the professor, but because of the material. I loathed reading about political science and authors of philosophy. Might as well have stuck me with a fork because I was done—or so I thought.

The more classes I took, the more I realized this was right up my alley after all. I discovered "I" could make a difference and wanted to make a difference, but I struggled with how to get my voice to the public. I wanted to talk about many topics, like one paper I authored in class: "Why does Congress pass laws for the citizens, but doesn't follow them?"

For example, Congress passed a law stating buildings will be accessible for the disabled, yet how many buildings in the Washington, DC capital area are not accessible to the disabled? Why is there a law to protect whistleblowers in the federal government, but not for the White House staff? Why is there a double standard for the lawmakers who make the laws for the citizens they represent?

With the knowledge I was gaining about policymaking, I started seeing tactics that the state and federal governments were using to block minority votes in the election of 2016. Many things were happening across the United States, and it seemed like much of America did not know. For example, states were closing voting locations that supported predominantly black neighborhoods, resulting in blacks having to travel greater distances to cast their votes on Election Day. Then when it was time to vote, Florida, Maryland, and South Carolina conveniently did not have enough voting machines or poll workers in predominantly black precincts. This resulted in voters standing in lines for hours, but this time, not only were heavily populated black counties affected, but all the citizens within the same precinct.[3] Immediately after President Obama won a second term in 2012, Virginia's state Republicans underhandedly voted to pass the redistricting measure that positioned them to take control of the Virginia Senate in 2015. This happened in the absence of Senator Henry Marsh, a Democrat and civil rights leader who attended the inaugural festivities. Prior to Senator Marsh attending the inaugural, the vote on the floor was a twenty-twenty split; however, the Republicans knew his absence

---

3   Christopher Famighetti, "Long Voting Lines: Explained," *Brennan Center for Justice*, November 4, 2016.

would give them the one vote they needed.[4] This, too, was probably happening across America.

I didn't know a great deal about what was happening, but I knew I wanted to investigate further. This drive to discover how minority voters were being disenfranchised led me to write my capstone paper on this very topic. The more I researched, the more I discovered and the angrier I became because the state and the federal governments were either passing and/or upholding laws, twisting the meaning of the Constitution, and coming up with excuses to justify passing such laws.

The Voting Rights Act (VRA) of 1965 solidified the Fifteenth Amendment, guaranteeing, again, citizens the right to vote regardless of color or race, mainly black men. The VRA consists of thirteen sections, of which sections four and five are most important.

Section 4 explains the "coverage formula," which questions if states known for implementing "tests or devices" still maintained them as of November 1, 1964, mainly unlawful laws preventing black men from voting. These states, under section five, were required to seek preclearance because of their past practices to suppress the black man's vote.[5] Preclearance means "those states needed approval in advance by a federal court or Department of Justice before enacting changes to the

---

4   Morgan Whitaker, "Virginia Republicans Celebrate Inauguration with Gerrymandering," *MSNBC News*, January 22, 2013.

5   The United States Department of Justice, "Section 4 of the Voting Rights Act," accessed September 12, 2020.

voting regulations."[6] As you will learn in Chapter One, black men faced several types of harassment or voter suppression.

In 2013, section 4(b), the coverage formula, faced a major defeat in the Supreme Court when it ruled in a five-to-four vote that it was unconstitutional to use the coverage formula.[7] As you will read and learn in Chapter Two, states immediately began implementing new obstacles and tactics to block and suppress the black vote without obtaining approval, i.e., by requiring state-issued Identification and now purging voters for not voting.

During graduation, the speaker charged us to make a difference. I cried because it was as if God was telling me, "*You have always been the voice of the underdog. I have given you an opportunity to attend this great institution to learn about policymaking, the good and the bad, and it is your responsibility to make a difference.*" Since then, I have had a desire to educate my black people on the importance of voting.

WHY THE BLACK VOTE IS IMPORTANT

I wanted to write not just your typical book on voting, but why it is so important. In my thirst to educate blacks about the tactics our government uses to disenfranchise our votes, it dawned on me many blacks, young and old, told me they do not vote because they don't think their vote matters. Know

6   Chris Bondi, "The Voting Rights Act: What is Preclearance?," *NEWS-MAX*, November 9, 2015.

7   ACLU, "Supreme Court Strikes Down Current Coverage Formula to Voting Rights Act," press release, June 25, 2013.

this, and I repeat—If your vote does not matter, why is our government doing so much to stop you from voting? Since you don't think your vote is important, my next question to you is this: When you decide not to vote, whatever the reason, *aren't you, too, disenfranchising our community's interests?*

Black votes do matter! I feel it is my responsibility to ensure every black person is educated on the numerous ways our government disenfranchised the black vote in the past, sees the tactics of the present, and pays attention to identify them in the future. This book discusses the past and present tactics used by the government to block black votes; the Civil Rights Act of 1964 and Voting Rights Act of 1965, and why they were needed to supplement the Fourteenth and Fifteenth Amendments; why all elections are important, especially the local ones; a few issues concerning the black community; and our responsibility to register, know our status, and *vote*!

In 2008, 138 years after the ratification of the Fifteenth Amendment, the United States of America made history by electing its first African American president, President Barack Hussein Obama. This resulted in an emergence of new tactics in an effort to not only suppress black votes but all minority votes for the 2012 presidential election.

During an interview with the *National Journal* on October 23, 2010, Senate Republican Leader Mitch McConnell openly stated, "The single most important thing we want to achieve is for President Obama to be a one-term president."[8] This

---

8   Glenn Kessler, "When Did Mitch McConnell Say He Wanted to Make Obama a One-Term President?" *The Washington Post*, January 11, 2017.

was the beginning of new tactics to disenfranchise and discourage blacks from voting. Those who tried to block our votes were scared of how much we could achieve for our communities with our votes. In light of these efforts, the people of the United States reelected President Obama for a second term. This is a prime example of how powerful the black vote is because without it, President Obama would not have won two terms.

It is time to fight back and make it known we are not okay with what our government is doing to deter us from voting. It is not okay that we have to maneuver a deliberately complicated system just to exercise our constitutional right to vote. While blacks have a history of voting for Democrats, we must exercise our right to vote, and not necessarily for the Democratic Party, but on the issues plaguing our communities and the party whose agenda aligns with ours.

When blacks do not vote, we are sending a message to our government at all levels that we do not care. This makes it easier for governments to disenfranchise us. Not only that, but we are demonstrating self-disenfranchisement because we are saying we hate our community just as much as those who are trying to stop us from voting. Per the *Urban Dictionary*, self-disenfranchisement is "the act of voting so irresponsibly, or voting for such individuals whose competence level is so inadequate, that one effectively cancels out their own vote, rendering the entire voting process meaningless for said individual."[9]

---

9 *Urban Dictionary*. s.v. "Self-Disenfranchisement," accessed March 12, 2020.

Allow me to add to that definition. When we do not take voting seriously, the issues affecting our community are not brought to the forefront of elected officials. Why do you think other cultures get what they want, mainly the white race? They get what they want because they make their issues known to their local, state, and national leaders; however, they do it in the most powerful way there is: They vote, and they get results!

Do you wonder why the trash dumps or industry-contaminated wastes are in the backyards of black neighborhoods? It is because whites made it known they do not want them in theirs. Let's face it, the laws are not written with blacks in mind, unless it is a law to lock us up, stop us from voting, or hinder progression in this America. Our communities have what we have because we decided not to vote for whatever the reason. Not voting leads to our communities getting the leftovers, if any exist. Not voting means our communities do not care, just offer lip service. Lip service equals No Service, which equals Self-Disenfranchisement, which equals Self-Hatred. Yet we blame everyone but ourselves.

When we vote, we are using our power to make changes at all levels that impact us directly or indirectly. The information in this book is not new, and I know politics do not interest everyone because for most of my life, they did not interest me. I get it. My intent is to make it as clear as daylight, or as Joe Madison says, "Put it where the goats can get it."[10] I hope this book inspires all readers to hunger to learn more about voting suppression in America and make a lifelong

____

10   Joe Madison, SiriusXM, *Urban View*, Channel 126, 2015, accessed 2015

commitment to vote in each and every election because black votes do matter. We need black history all year, not just in February. History books should be rewritten ensuring we are on the right side of history. Unfortunately, President Trump stated he will defund educational districts that teach about the 1619 Project, a project telling our side of history from the moment our ancestors were first trafficked to Virginia.[11]

"If you don't know what happened behind you, you won't know what is happening in front of you." From 2014 to 2016, while commuting to the Springfield, Virginia Metro to attend class at Georgetown University, I listened to Sirius XM Radio, *Urban View*, Channel 126, 6:00 a.m., and stumbled across Mr. Joe Madison, the Black Eagle, activist, black historian, and full of our history, who at first I thought was a total asshole. The more I listened to him, though, the more I understood exactly where he was coming from and what he meant. I appreciated his candor on issues affecting black Americans, our past, and potential outcomes if we didn't become more involved.

Monday through Friday, he teaches black history, past and present, and how to "read with a third eye and listen with a third ear."[12] This means, when people say things to you, when you hear something on the television, or when you read about it, pay attention to the information that is being channeled into your brain. Use what you know to decipher the information. Don't accept any and everything someone tells you

---

11   Josephine Harvey, "Trump Threatens to Yank Funding from Schools That Teach 1619 Project," *HuffPost*, September 6, 2020.

12   Joe Madison, SiriusXM, *Urban View*, Channel 126, accessed 2015.

or what you read without deciphering or researching it. In essence, become an investigator, so to speak, by dissecting what you hear and/or read. We cannot have an intelligent discussion on any issue if we are not informed.

I learned and continue to learn a great deal by listening to his morning show, oftentimes angry as all get-out by what I hear and learn as it relates to blacks and the political system, realizing there is so much I do not know. So, if we don't know what happened before us, we will not know what is happening right in front of our very eyes. This statement resonates deep within me. Mr. Madison always asks this question on the show, "What are *you* going to do?" Well, I've decided to write a book to expose a minute fraction of our history on suppressing the black vote. Let's discover, together, how we got here and how to be part of the solution.

PART I:

SUPPRESSION, SUPPLEMENTS, AND ELECTIONS

CHAPTER 1

PAST TACTICS TO DISENFRANCHISE THE BLACK VOTE

———

"How many bubbles are in a bar of soap?" or "How many jellybeans are in the jar?"

Imagine being asked this question in order to register to vote, to change your community, to determine your future, or to exercise your constitutional right to vote. My mother, who was born in 1933, said these were questions asked on a mandatory literacy test to register to vote. It didn't matter what response was given; it was always the wrong one.

We must know the many ways our government disenfranchises the black vote. We must educate ourselves on how our government creates laws to prevent, hinder, and block black votes. I like this quote by Dr. Martin Luther King, Jr.:

"Nothing in all the world is more dangerous than sincere ignorance and conscientious stupidity."[13] Which one are you?

This chapter focuses on the past tactics against the black man.

DISENFRANCHISEMENT

There are two types of disenfranchisement: direct and indirect. *Direct disenfranchisement* is used in connection with race, voting rights, and segregation. It refers to "actions that explicitly prevent people from voting or having their votes counted."[14] *Indirect disenfranchisement* "attempts to prevent people's votes from having an impact on political outcomes by gerrymandering, redistricting, ballot box stuffing, stripping elected officials of their powers," and more recently, removing voters from the registrar's list.[15] Our government used, and still uses, numerous tactics to block the black vote. This issue is so important it is divided into two parts: Chapter One, Past Tactics to Disenfranchise the Black Vote, and Chapter Two, Recent Tactics to Disenfranchise the Black Vote. Let's start with the past tactics to block black votes.

It is imperative to understand why your vote is so important. If it weren't, ask yourself why would there be a constant effort on the part of our government to stop the black vote? While doing my research on the topic of voting and disenfranchisement, I was amazed at how states and the Supreme Court

---

13   Terry Levine, "Sincere Ignorance and Conscientious Stupidity," *Noggin*, July 11, 2011.

14   Direct Disenfranchisement, *Bing*, accessed April 3, 2020.

15   Indirect Disenfranchisement, *Bing*, accessed April 3, 2020.

passed laws violating the Fifteenth Amendment. Remember, black men were granted the right to vote when the Fifteenth Amendment was ratified; however, at that time, women could not vote. Please understand women were not allowed to vote until Congress passed the Nineteenth Amendment on June 4, 1919, and ratified it August 18, 1920.[16]

The southern white legislators were not happy one bit when black men were allowed to vote and did everything in their power, successfully might I add, to prevent the black man from voting. That is how powerful the black vote was then and is today. Some of you may or may not have heard of the past tactics and may find them a bit shocking, while for others, this brings back memories because you experienced it or heard parents or grandparents speak of them. Think about it; white legislators could not fathom a black man, a former slave, who was not even considered a whole man, but three-fifths of a person, being equal to them.

Unlawful tactics to disenfranchise and suppress the black vote date as far back as the Reconstruction Era (1865 to 1877). Once slavery was abolished in the United States by ratifying the Thirteenth Amendment (1865), former slaves were then considered citizens by the passage of the Fourteenth Amendment (1868), and finally granted the right to vote when the Fifteenth Amendment was ratified in 1870. Ratifying these three amendments aimed to help freed slaves transition from slavery to freedom, but it was highly contested by the former Confederate states.

---

16   National Archives, "The Constitution: Amendments 11-27," accessed April 4, 2020.

Ratifying these three amendments also meant blacks, rather former slaves, were no longer under whites' control; however, this did not last long because the southern states repealed all of the Reconstruction Acts created by radical Republicans, the party once headed by President Abraham Lincoln. Interesting how during this time, the Republicans were considered radical for wanting to help blacks. "The Reconstruction Act was enacted by the US Congress between 1867 and 1868 and consisted of several acts and supplemental legislation after the Civil War."[17] The purpose of the supplemental legislation was to keep the southern states in check by protecting black citizens with equal rights and voting rights.

There were four Reconstruction Acts to protect blacks. The legislation 1) "established military districts in the South; 2) demanded new state constitutions, approved by Congress, for all southern states rejoining the Union; 3) required that all men in all southern states be granted the right to vote; and 4) required that states ratify the Fourteenth Amendment, which established blacks as legal citizens, as a condition of readmission to the Union."[18] When the Fifteenth Amendment was passed in 1870, a small percentage of freed slaves, primarily in the North, had voting privileges. During Reconstruction, which lasted about ten years, blacks were mainly Republicans, belonging to the party of Lincoln, and took full advantage of their voting rights by supporting Republican officials. Naturally, blacks elected other blacks into office.

---

17   "The Reconstruction Act," *American Historama*, updated January 9, 2018, accessed April 4, 2020.

18   Ibid

"During Reconstruction, sixteen black men served in Congress and two thousand black men served in elected local, state, and federal positions."[19] High-ranking black Republicans during this period held positions as state legislators, governors, and US senators. Congressmen Robert Smalls from South Carolina and John Lynch from Mississippi, and Governor P.B.S. Pinchback from Louisiana were among many black politicians during the 1870s and early 1880s. This would have been a piece of black history I would have loved to learn about during high school. Oh, wait, I remember the history books were whitewashed—absent of any meaningful black success stories.

By the mid-1870s, with the support of a new administration, the Democratic Party regained much of its former congressional power. Angry white Southerners were seeking redemption for the loss of the Civil War, and their most pressing concern was a "struggle for mastery" once again over freed slaves. In their effort to return to a white supremacy status quo, they took on disenfranchisement as a political process that took only a few decades to accomplish. To prevent blacks from enjoying these new rights and political victories, white Southerners began manipulating the elections in various ways. Let's explore the numerous ways the elections were manipulated.

Fraud: Fraud was a form of indirect disenfranchisement. It was one sure way to guarantee the black vote did not count by practicing electoral fraud. This was accomplished

---

19   Rick Jervis, "Black Americans Got the Right to Vote 150 Years Ago, but Voter Suppression Still a Problem," *USA Today*, February 3, 2020.

by something called "ballot box stuffing," where whites who were charged as election inspectors would throw out non-Democratic votes or count them for the Democrats even when cast for the Republican. Of course, this was normal in southern states before the legalization of illegal means of disenfranchisement was entrenched. "Between 1880 and 1901, Congress, doing the right thing, allowed twenty-six Republican or Populist congressional candidates who had been 'defeated' through electoral fraud to take their seats as elected officials.[20]

Using the Enforcement Act of 1870, prosecutors brought indictments against two inspectors of elections in Kentucky for refusing to receive and count the vote of a black elector in a city election. In this case, the Supreme Court dismissed the indictments in US v. Reese, 92 US 214 (1875). Here, the Supreme Court felt the election officials exceeded Congress's power to regulate elections. Really?[21]

The provisions stated that "officials shall be punished for failure to count the votes of eligible electors, when the Fifteenth Amendment granted Congress only the power to punish officials for depriving electors of the right to vote on account of race."[22] Although electoral fraud remained common in the South, those practicing voter fraud were not seen in a positive

---

20 Morgan J. Kousser, *Shaping of Southern Politics. Suffrage Restriction and the Establishment of the One-Party South, 1880-1910*, (Yale University Press, 1974).

21 "United States v. Reese Et Al," Cornell Law School, Legal Information Institute, accessed April 14, 2020.

22 Morgan J. Kousser, *Shaping of Southern Politics*.

light among the public, which, in turn, motivated white Southerners to turn to legal means of disenfranchisement.

Violence: In the South, a form of direct disenfranchisement utilized before redemption was violence. Redemption is a term used by white Southerners that refers to reversing the South back to a conservative Democratic party rule after Reconstruction (1865 to 1877), after the Civil War. Recall, one of the Reconstruction Acts included military district established laws; therefore, the South was occupied by federal forces, and the state governments were dominated by radical Republicans.

What kind of violent behaviors did black voters experience? Some of the same things during the 1960s, which included verbal harassment or physical assault to prevent them from casting their ballots or even reaching the polls. Voter intimidation via violent threats and terror campaigns occurred without any legal intervention.[23] Last, but definitely not least, they were killed for exercising their lawful right to vote as in the case of US v. Cruikshank 92 US 542 (1875) in 1873, "when over one hundred blacks and three whites were killed in Colfax, Louisiana, by a band of whites because they assembled to defend Republican officeholders."[24]

---

23 "A Brief History of African American Voter Disenfranchisement," *US Slave* (blog), June 23, 2013, accessed April 9, 2020.

24 Eric Foner, *Reconstruction: America's Unfinished Revolution*, 1989, 531, quoted in J. Morgan Kousser, *The Shaping of Southern Politics: Suffrage Restriction and the Establishment of the One-Party South, 1880-1910*, (Yale University Press, 1974) and Samuel Issacharoff, Pamela Karlan and

Even though federal prosecutors indicted three of the accused under the Enforcement Act of 1870, which prohibited individuals from doing the following: "to injure, oppress, threaten, or intimidate any citizen, with intent to prevent or hinder [the] exercise and enjoyment of any [constitutional or federally granted] right or privilege," the US Supreme Court dismissed the indictment.[25] As you can see, justice truly was blind then, like today, when the law knows who the whites are who killed black men, but they are not charged. In this case, black men were killed for defending Republican officeholders.

This is a time in our history when the Supreme Court ignores, overlooks, or exercises racist acts and decides to rule in favor of the three white defendants, knowing they violated the Enforcement Act. The Supreme Court case of US v. Cruikshank basically allowed the exact circumstances the Enforcement Act was meant to combat. This decision allowed violence and degradation of rights to freed slaves. "Cruikshank rendered national prosecution of crimes against blacks virtually impossible, and gave a green light to acts of terror where local officials either could not or would not enforce the law."[26]

<hr>

Richard Pildes, *The Law of Democracy* (University of Michigan: Foundation Press, 1998), accessed April 9, 2020.

25 Debo Adegbile, "The Killing of Jimmy Lee Jackson," *The Marshall Project*, January 27, 2015.

26 Eric Forner, *Reconstruction: America's Unfinished Revolution*, quoted in Debo Adegbile, "The Killing of Jimmy Lee Jackson," *The Marshall Project*, February 27, 2015.

Poll Tax: A poll tax was a form of direct disenfranchisement. Georgia initiated poll taxes in 1871, requiring all citizens to pay back taxes before being permitted to vote, and later in 1877, making the taxes cumulative.[27] By 1904, every former Confederate state followed suit.

At the time, the taxes were between one to two dollars per year. Obviously, many poor blacks and white sharecroppers could not afford this amount of money. Since they could not afford to pay the poll taxes, they were not allowed to vote, thus reducing the overall turnout by 16 to 28 percent, and black turnout in half.[28] The purpose of the tax was plainly to disenfranchise black voters, not to collect revenue, since no state brought prosecutions against any individual for failure to pay the tax.

In 1937, a white man brought suit against Georgia's poll tax, alleging it violated the Fourteenth Amendment and the Nineteenth Amendment, which discriminated based on sex, the Supreme Court case Breedlove v. Suttles, 302 US 277 (1937).[29] During this time, if women were not registered to vote, they did not have to pay poll taxes. Once again, the

---

27 J. Morgan Kousser, *Shaping of Southern Politics*, 26, quoted in "Techniques of Direct Disenfranchisement," *University of Michigan*, accessed April 9, 2020.

28 J. Morgan Kousser, *The Shaping of Southern Politics: Suffrage Restriction and the Establishment of the One-Party South, 1880-1910*, Historical Publications, Miscellany Series, 67-8.

29 "Breedlove v. Suttles, 302 U.S. 277 (1937)," *JUSTIA US Supreme*, Case Law, Supreme Court, Volume 302.

Supreme Court was blind and upheld Georgia's decision to allow poll taxes as a prerequisite to voting.

Although the case of Harper v. Virginia Board of Elections ultimately reversed the Breedlove v. Suttles decision, and passage of the Twenty-Fourth Amendment prohibited the poll tax in federal elections, that still wasn't enough to prevent a last-ditch attempt to burden the right to vote with a tax. It took the Voting Rights Act of 1965 to prohibit poll taxes in state elections. Then, the Supreme Court independently declared poll taxes an unconstitutional violation of the equal protection clause of the Fourteenth Amendment in Harper v. Virginia State Bd. of Elections, 383 US 663 (1966).[30] While this tactic was clearly aimed at blacks, it also affected poor whites.

Literacy Tests: Literacy tests were a form of direct disenfranchisement. The first state to prohibit blacks from voting was South Carolina by adopting the use of the "eight-box" ballot in 1882. This required voters to put ballots for separate offices in separate boxes. If a voter put a ballot for the governor's race in the box for the senate seat, election officials threw it out. The order of the boxes was continuously shuffled so that voters who could read were not allowed to help voters who could not read by arranging their ballots in the proper order. The adoption of the secret ballot constituted another implicit literacy test since it prohibited anyone from assisting an illiterate voter in casting his vote.[31]

---

30 "Harper v. Virginia Board of Election - Poll Tax Law Violated Equal Protection Clause," *Constitutional Law Reporter,* accessed April 5, 2020.

31 "Techniques of Direct Disenfranchisement," University of Michigan, accessed April 19, 2020.

Two years later in 1890, southern states began adopting explicit literacy tests to disenfranchise voters. For example, one of the questions on Mississippi's literacy test required applicants to write a section of Mississippi's constitution, and then explain the meaning of it. Louisiana's literacy tests were clearly designed to ensure black voters could not register by asking thirty of the dumbest questions, which had to be answered in ten minutes, and one wrong response meant you failed. Take a look at one of the questions: "Write every other word in this first line and print every third word in the same line (original type smaller and first line ended at comma) but capitalize the fifth word that you write."[32] Talk about a bunch of bull. This ensured every black man attempting to register to vote failed!

"This had a large differential racial impact, since 40 to 60 percent of blacks were illiterate, compared to 8 to 18 percent of whites. Poor, illiterate whites did not like the tests, realizing they, too, were disenfranchised."[33] So, to try to satisfy them, the southern states adopted something called an "understanding clause" or a "grandfather clause." This would allow those voters who couldn't pass the literacy test an opportunity to vote if they could demonstrate their understanding of the meaning of a passage in the constitution to the satisfaction of the registrar, or if they were descendants from someone eligible to vote in 1867. This was the year before

---

32 Rebecca Onion, "Take the Impossible 'Literacy' Test Louisiana Gave Black Voters in the 1960s," *SLATE*, June 28, 2013, accessed April 9, 2020.

33 "Techniques of Direct Disenfranchisement," University of Michigan, accessed April 9, 2020.

blacks attained the franchise.[34] Remember when I discussed reading with a third eye? Did you catch, "to the satisfaction of the registrar?" This means if the registrar, a white man, felt the response was the right one, then he would allow the black man to register to vote.

It is clear this was a deliberate act in that it solidified the fact that black men were ineligible to vote through the understanding clause. While southern states were attempting to screw the black men, ironically, illiterate whites also felt the impact of the literacy tests since some of the understanding and grandfather clauses expired after a few years, and some whites were reluctant to expose their illiteracy by publicly resorting to them.[35]

Black voters attempting to pass the literacy test were faced with some of the dumbest questions as a way to stop the black vote. My mother, who was born in 1933, told me of a question blacks were asked on the literacy test: "How many bubbles are in a bar of soap?" As silly and ridiculous as this sounds, it was a question asked by the registrar to keep blacks from voting. Another question asked was "How many jellybeans are in this jar?" No matter the response, blacks attempting to register to vote never gave the correct answer. Congress abolished literacy tests in the South with the Voting Rights Act of 1965, and nationwide in 1970.[36]

---

34   Ibid.

35   Ibid.

36   Ibid.

<u>**White Primaries:**</u> White primaries were a form of direct disenfranchisement, limiting blacks from political influence. After Reconstruction (1865 to 1877), naturally, white Southerners did other tactics to minimize the economic, political, and social opportunities of freed slaves and their descendants. A primary is an election within a political party where they select their candidate for president. In the late 1800s and early 1900s, states started replacing party conventions with primaries, which became "white" primaries to specifically deny black voters the right to participate in the political process.[37]

By this time, the existence of the Republican Party was pretty much dissolved, mainly by white voters, but not by black voters. Eventually, their numbers got significantly smaller because of the new laws which had an impact on disenfranchising their votes. If blacks wanted to continue participating in the political process, they would have to become Democrats. Well, the Democratic Party was not about to let that happen, so many states decided to create a rule preventing them from becoming a member of the party. The state legislatures worked in concert with the party, closing the primaries to everyone except party members. Well, all the party members were white, another example of how the state government sided with another unlawful law.

Once again, in 1921, the Supreme Court ruled favorably "in Newberry v. United States, 256 US 232, 41 S. Ct. 469, 65 L. Ed. 913, stating political parties were private organizations, not

---

37 "Techniques of Direct Disenfranchisement," University of Michigan, accessed April 9, 2020.

part of the government election apparatus."[38] This is another example of the Supreme Court (or justice) being blind, and a prime example of incorrect interpretation of the law to benefit those in power—white Southerners. This is also an example of illegally legalizing discrimination of the right of blacks to vote, violating the Fourteenth Amendment's equal protection clause.

In many subsequent cases of this tactic, the Supreme Court ruled against the fair treatment of black voters, but finally, the Supreme Court ruled that federal governments could regulate party primaries to prevent voter fraud. White primaries were deemed a violation of the Fifteenth Amendment by not allowing blacks the right to vote based on race.[39]

<u>Restrictive and Arbitrary Registration Practices:</u> Restrictive and arbitrary registration practices were methods of direct disenfranchisement. If black men were literate and financially able to take care of themselves, racist registration practices were created to make their efforts to vote miserable. "Southern states made registration difficult by requiring frequent re-registration, long terms of residence in a district, registration at inconvenient times (e.g., planting season), provision of information unavailable to many blacks (e.g., street addresses, when black neighborhoods lacked street names and numbers), and so forth."[40] Once blacks managed to qual-

---

38   "White Primary – Party, Court, African, and Americans," *JRank Articles*, accessed April 10, 2020.

39   Ibid.

40   "Techniques of Direct Disenfranchisement," University of Michigan, accessed April 9, 2020.

ify to vote even under these measures, registrars would use their discretion to deny them the vote anyway.

Alabama's Constitution of 1901 was explicitly designed to disenfranchise blacks by such restrictive and fraudulent means. Despite this, Jackson Giles, a black janitor, qualified for the vote under Alabama's constitution. He brought suit against Alabama on behalf of himself and seventy-five thousand similarly qualified blacks who had been arbitrarily denied the right to register. The Supreme Court rejected his claim in Giles v. Harris, 189 US 475 (1903).[41] As you can see, yet again, the Supreme Court was intentionally blind and siding with white Alabamian lawmakers.

Not to be moved by the decision, Giles then filed suit for damages against the registrars in state court and petitioned the court to order the registrars to register him. The state court dismissed his complaints. The reason Giles' case was such a challenge is that in the Alabama Constitution of 1901, Alabama had a Board of Registrars who gave the literacy tests. They were the ones who determined if one passed the test or not. No matter how smart and well prepared blacks were for the test, the Board of Registrars would tell them they failed it, and of course, the test black men took was harder than the test white men took.

---

41   Ibid.

* * *

QUESTIONS?

If you lived during this time frame, knowing you had the legal right to vote based on the passage of the Fifteenth Amendment, what would you do if you were denied that right? Would you have had the same courage as many blacks and whites who lost their lives had to stand up to injustice?

CHAPTER 2

RECENT TACTICS TO DISENFRANCHISE BLACK VOTES

The US Constitution does not explicitly state that if you don't exercise your right to vote, you lose it, so why are people being purged from the rolls for not voting?

In 2008, 138 years after the ratification of the Fifteenth Amendment, the United States of America made history by electing its first African American president, President Barack Hussein Obama. After the 2008 election, Senate Republican Leader Mitch McConnell openly stated the party's goal was to make President Obama a one-term president.[42] This resulted in the emergence of new tactics to not only suppress black votes but all minority votes for the 2012 presidential election. However, despite new tactics, the people

---

42 Glenn Kessler, "When did Mitch McConnell Say He Wanted to Make Obama a One-Term President?" *The Washington Post*, January 11, 2017.

of the United States reelected President Barack Obama for a second term.

The open and blatant disrespect for President Obama by Congress exposed deep-seated racism. In the last chapter, I defined two types of disenfranchisement: direct and indirect. "*Direct disenfranchisement* is used in connection with race, voting rights, and segregation. It refers to actions that explicitly prevent people from voting or having their votes counted."[43] Most of the examples in Chapter One were direct disenfranchisement. This chapter lists examples of indirect disenfranchisement. "*Indirect disenfranchisement* attempts to prevent people's votes from having an impact on political outcomes by gerrymandering, redistricting, ballot box stuffing, stripping elected officials of their powers, and removing voters from the registrar's list."[44]

It is important that I reiterate the two types of disenfranchisement because once you can identify the characteristics, you will say, "Ahh yeah, that is what she was talking about." My goal is to help you see systemic racism by our government through their actions, and for what? Power. Their greed, selfishness, and disdain for those not running in their circle reminds me of Mark 8:36: "For what shall it profit a man, if he shall gain the whole world, and lose his own soul?" (KJV). It also reminds me of Ecclesiastes 6:7: "All a man's labor is for his mouth and the appetite is not satisfied." (KJV). This is ideal because politicians will do anything to stay in power and to satisfy their insatiable power-loving appetites.

---

43   Direct Disenfranchisement, *Bing*, accessed April 9, 2020.

44   Indirect Disenfranchisement, *Bing*, accessed April 9, 2020.

VOTER IDENTIFICATION

Voter identification (ID) is direct disenfranchisement, which attempts to prevent one from participating in the election process by not having the new government-issued identification. There are many states with strict voting registration laws, but the laws in Wisconsin are the most restrictive. The moment the US Supreme Court determined section 4(b) of the Voting Rights Acts was unconstitutional, Wisconsin was the first state to implement voter identification and Real ID in 2016. Citizens who wanted a Real ID needed to produce all of these forms of identification:

- Proof of name and date of birth; for example, a certified US birth certificate, valid passport, or certificate of naturalization.
- Proof of identity (usually a document with a signature or photo).
- Proof of Wisconsin residency.
- Proof of US citizenship, legal permanent resident status, legal conditional resident status, or legal temporary visitor status.
- Your social security number.

Also, in the state of Wisconsin, you cannot have both forms of ID; it's either a driver's license or ID card. If you want an ID card, then you must turn in your driver's license and give up your driving privileges.[45]

---

45   State of Wisconsin Department of Transportation, Department of Motor Vehicles, accessed April 2, 2020.

One African American gentleman, Mr. Eddie L. Holloway, Jr., voted in every election since he was eighteen years old. This changed, however, when Wisconsin implemented the voter ID law. Unfortunately, his name was not recorded properly on his birth certificate; it had Eddie Junior Holloway, which did not match with the name on his social security card and expired Illinois photo ID, Eddie L. Holloway, Jr. "He became severely disabled, unemployed, and homeless," resulting in him not being able to get a Wisconsin photo ID after getting the runaround about the required documents (listed above) needed to prove his identity.

Not to be defeated, he traveled for four hours to Illinois to get a copy of his high school and shot records. When he returned, he found out he needed his social security statement, not the card. Now, why wasn't this provided as one of the mandatory forms of identification? After getting all of the required documents, he was then told he had to pay to have his birth certificate changed, which he could not afford, so he gave up.[46] Let this be a lesson for you. If you do not have a copy of your birth certificate, get one! If you have one, make sure your name is spelled correctly.

I say this, but guess what, my name is incorrect on my birth certificate! My whole life, most people spell my name the way they've seen it, without actually looking at the spelling. My social security card has the correct spelling. Hmm, maybe I have some homework too—to research the cost to change my name on my birth certificate to the correct spelling.

---

46   Kathleen Wong, "This Wisconsin Man Brought Three Forms of Identification to the Polls and Still Couldn't Vote," *Yahoo News,* April 14, 2016.

By October 1, 2021, everyone must have a Real ID, and that is only one form of identification. Chances are that some of you have yet to get a Real ID.

REAL IDENTIFICATION

Real ID is a hot topic lately. The REAL ID Act was initiated after the United States World Trade Center Twin Towers in New York suffered a terrorist attack on September 11, 2001, now called 9/11. The purpose is an "effort to stop fraudulence by terrorist organizations to create driver's licenses and ensure secure identification started at home, the United States." Anyone who does not have a Real ID will not be allowed access to federal facilities, nuclear power plants, or board federally regulated commercial aircraft."[47]

The Real ID is replacing the drivers' license. It looks like a regular driver's license, but with a star on the top to distinguish it. The star indicates the driver's license is more secure with fewer chances of being forged. The initial deadline for everyone to have a Real ID was October 1, 2020, but the deadline was extended to October 2021 due to COVID-19. For those with a passport, the Real ID is great because it can be used in lieu of carrying your passport.

Having a Real ID is to ensure you are who you say you are, but often when poor people and minorities attempt to get the proper identification, there seems to be a glitch. First, you must show proof of residency. To do that, citizens need the following documents:

---

47   Department of Homeland Security, "Real ID," accessed April 16, 2020.

An energy provider bill (what if you are renting a room), bank
statement (what if people prefer to use something like Green
Dot), tax assessment (what if you are not a homeowner and
don't own a car because you live in the city where public transportation is the preferred mode of travel), photo ID (mind you,
this must be government-issued), mortgage statement (previous statement answers this), certificate of voter registration (if
I am not mistaken, you might just need two forms of government-issued identification), or any correspondence between
you and a government authority regarding the receipt of benefits, such as a pension (what if I am too young to receive a pension), unemployment benefits (I have a job), housing benefits
(I don't get housing benefits from the government), etcetera.[48]

So, what is the problem, you ask. Besides the rebuttals above,
what does a homeless person do? Chances are they will not
have these documents; therefore, they can't register to vote.
If I am trying to get a driver's license or a state ID in Virginia,
I need two proofs of current residency, one proof of social
security number, and one proof of name change, if applicable.
This impacts the homeless, college students, and ex-felons.

REDISTRICTING/GERRYMANDERING

Redistricting is indirect disenfranchisement. It takes place
every ten years after completion of the United States Census
to prepare for the next election. Redistricting is a federally
governed process designed to ensure congressional districts

---

48   The DMV.ORG, "The DMV Made Simple," accessed April 16, 2020.

adequately reflect the shifts in population distribution.[49] You've seen commercials and advertisements for completing the Census so funding can be poured into your community for transportation, etcetera. It's deeper than that. The US Constitution requires each representative in Congress to represent an equal number of citizens; therefore, a census is done to determine the number of citizens. This information is then used to apportion seats to each state.

However, on December 8, 2015, the Supreme Court heard a redistricting case presented by Sue Evenwel and Edward Pfenninger, arguing that representation should be based on those who actually vote—one person, one vote, and not the total population. Amazing how in years past, the Fourteenth Amendment could not protect freed slaves, but when it was convenient for those who did not want the total population represented, it was used as an argument in Texas. The argument was that "the Equal Protection Clause of the Fourteenth Amendment required *voters*, rather than *residents*, to be used as the denominator."[50]

Instead, on April 2, 2016, the Supreme Court unanimously decided against basing representation on the number of registered voters. The opinion authored by Justice Ruth Bader Ginsberg, commonly known as RBG, concluded the current process is and has been working fine for decades: "The Supreme Court will not stand the Equal Protection Clause

---

49   Michael Holtz, "Redistricting or Gerrymandering? N.C. Dispute Embodies National Debate," *The Christian Science Monitor*, March 11, 2016.

50   Scott Lemieux, "Equal Representation Won a Qualified Victory at the Supreme Court," *The New Republic*, April 4, 2016.

on its head by requiring states to dilute minority representation."[51] This would have been a major defeat for voters' rights if the Supreme Court sided with this interpretation. In this case, justice was not blind and, in my opinion, the Court ruled properly.

Think about this for a moment. If this were passed by the Supreme Court, representation would have only been for those who are of age to vote or eligible to vote, who actually voted, and many blacks and the poor tend to vote less often than whites. "One vote, one person" would promise Republicans a victory, again, only because it is known that most blacks tend not to show up to vote, and those who do tend to vote Democrat. If this passed, imagine the rest of the population who would not be represented—anyone under the age of eighteen, anyone over the age of eighteen but does not vote, people residing in America without full citizenship but have to take the Census, and ex-felons whose voting rights have not yet been reinstated although they completed their time and paid restitution. This would have primarily affected the minority communities in Texas, especially where the population is heavily Latino.

GERRYMANDERING

Gerrymandering is indirect disenfranchisement. It is in the same family as redistricting, as it refers to "the use of the redistricting process to unfairly disenfranchise specific

____

51   Ibid.

groups of people."[52] Political advantage includes drawing boundaries isolating low-income minority communities while favoring middle-class and affluent communities, resulting in a significant difference in funding for schools and other programs.

Gerrymandering also attempts to impact black votes. This is an example of an unsuccessful attempt by the Republicans to change the election outcome in 2012. After the United States Census of 2010, many states began redistricting and gerrymandering, drawing legislative boundaries to favor Republicans for the next election when Senator Barack Obama won the presidential election in 2008. The goal was to prevent him from serving a second term. It is important to understand that when a political party controls the state legislature, they redraw the boundaries based on the Census and previous elections. Their purpose was to ensure their party has the political advantage for future elections. As you know, President Obama won a second term.

Completing the 2020 Census is very important and required by law. The commercials indicate one reason it is done is to ensure you have public transportation in your neighborhood so you don't have to walk too far to or from the bus stop. But don't believe the hype. Pay attention because once the 2020 Census is completed, the district boundaries will be redrawn yet again and you will wonder why your children attend different schools. Now that I think about it, none of

---

52   Michael Holtz, "Redistricting or Gerrymandering? N.C. Dispute Embodies National Debate," *The Christian Science Monitor*, March 11, 2016.

my siblings and I attended the same high school! We were bused all over Columbus, Georgia.

INCARCERATION OF AFRICAN AMERICANS AND MINORITIES

The incarceration of African Americans and minorities is indirect disenfranchisement. In 2016, blacks were imprisoned at a higher rate than whites for the same crimes, or on trumped up charges. As of May 23, 2020, the Federal Bureau of Prisons' statistics show there are more whites in prison than African Americans, Asians, and Native Americans combined. Ironically, the Latino population is not listed.[53]

The Pew Research Center published an analysis of data from the Bureau of Justice Statistics. It showed that when President Obama left office, he had a smaller federal prison population than President Jimmy Carter, and used clemency more than any other president.[54] Of course, this is nothing to shout about, nor is it a victory, because anytime minorities are placed in jail, they have a hard time re-entering society to become productive citizens. More often than not, they return to the same streets and have a hard time getting employment, and most places will not rent to ex-felons. Those who have "learned their lesson" become discouraged. Then, when it is time to register to vote, if their state law has restrictions, they

---

53   Bureau of Federal Prisons, Statistics: Inmate Race, accessed September 16, 2020.

54   John Gramlich, Federal prison population fell during Obama's term, reversing recent trend, Pew Research Center, January 5, 2017.

have to request to have their voting rights reinstated, which can be an arduous process.

Remember, each state writes its own legislation about reinstating the voting rights to ex-felons, even when it comes to federal elections. What's most surprising is that only two states, Maine and Vermont, never revoke one's voting rights, even if the crime is a felony. Four states (Arizona for repeat offenders, Iowa, Kentucky, and certain felons in Mississippi) require the governor to reinstate voting rights. The remaining states allow ex-felons the right to vote once they have completed all of their sentence, i.e., served the mandated time, probation, parole, and/or paid financial restitution.[55] Herein lies another problem: When ex-felons complete their sentence and are allowed to vote, then they need a government-issued ID. This poses a hurdle because, after all, they have been locked up for a while. Their state ID will be out of date, and they will not have a Real ID, will be unable to get an apartment in their name, will not have utility bills in their name, and will not be paying property taxes, so how easy will it be to get the proper forms of identification to register to vote?

CLOSING VOTING LOCATIONS & ENDING EARLY VOTING

Another widespread tactic is the closing of voting locations, which is direct disenfranchisement. Since the June 2013 US Supreme Court decision to strike down part of the Voting

---

55   Tom Murse, "Where People Convicted of Felonies Can Vote in the U.S.," *ThoughtCo.*, updated September 12, 2020.

Rights Act of 1965—requiring certain states to get federal approval before changing their voting laws—many states closed approximately sixteen hundred voting locations. What are the states saying about the reasons for the closures? The reasons range from budgetary constraints to consolidating to one location in lieu of neighborhood locations. On the other hand, South Carolina has added forty-five locations since 2012.[56]

Why is this an issue? It is an issue because most of the locations were in minority neighborhoods. Closing voting locations in minority neighborhoods reduces the number of voters going to the polls for many reasons. They may not have personal transportation to drive to the voting location. Due to subpar jobs paying poverty salaries, they don't have extra money to afford an Über or cab ride to vote. The new voting location assigned to them may not be on the public transportation route.

Some voting locations did not have enough voting booths, causing people to stand in line for hours, as in the 2008 election in Florida, in which voters brought chairs. Voters were determined then, as they are now, to cast their vote despite the length of time they had to wait. However, closing voting locations in minority communities resulted in a lower voter turnout—by design. It is also thought that if minorities are sent to other locations, they could be met with intimidation, which may cause them to change their vote. For example, in Philadelphia, voters accused the pollsters of intimidation by

---

56   Andy Sullivan, "Southern U.S. States Have Closed 1,200 Polling Places in Recent Years: Rights Group," Reuters, September 10, 2019.

placing Bibles at each voting station.[57] What is not understood is we are not our parents or grandparents, and we cannot be intimidated.

More recently in Wisconsin, due to COVID-19, its one hundred eighty voting locations were reduced to five for the primaries because the Governor said it was safer, while wearing a mask and surgical gown. This, too, resulted in a significantly low number of voter turnout and long lines.[58] Remember, this is by design.

Why are the Republican governors playing down the COVID-19 virus while thousands of people are dying? Why are they politicizing this pandemic? Pay attention and watch. Once they are impacted by it, it will become real and then they will promote masks, distancing, and washing hands. A prime example is Republican Chris Christie, who now realizes he should have taken the virus more seriously but had a false sense of protection because the people he associated with were tested daily, something we cannot afford.[59] Mark my words, lawmakers do not change laws until they are impacted.

---

57   Matt Vasilogambros, "Polling Places in Black Communities Continue to Close Ahead of November Elections," *GOVERNING*, September 5, 2018.

58   John Oliver, "Voting by Mail." *Last Week Tonight with John Oliver*, HBO, May 31, 2020. YouTube. 19:11.

59   Tamar Lapin, "Chris Christie Says It Was 'Serious Failure' Not to Wear Mask at White House," *The New York Post*, September 21, 2020.

PURGING STATE VOTER REGISTRATIONS

Purging state voter registrations is direct disenfranchisement and the latest tactic. This first caught my attention after the race for governor in Atlanta, Georgia, between Democrat Stacey Abrams and Republican Brian Kemp. Kemp, at the time, was the Georgia Secretary of State and the overseer of the voter purge. Between 2012 and 2018, more than 1.4 million registrations were canceled. I had to research how voters could legally be purged from the rolls.

Purging voter rolls is common and done regularly because people move or die. The purges are driven by districts that once had to get preclearance by the federal government to change voting laws. Georgia is not the only state purging voters for not voting in a three-year period. The Brennan Center for Justice reports that between 2014 and 2016, over 17 million voters were purged.[60] I am still trying to wrap my head around a law that is more restrictive than the Fifteenth Amendment, which granted black men the same voting rights as white men, and the Nineteenth Amendment, which granted all women the same rights.

The purge doesn't mainly affect the minority community, but everyone, even conservative voters, when there is a flaw in the database. Once Ohio realized they had a flaw when active conservative voters were removed from the registry; now they are going to wait until after the 2020 election.[61]

---

60 Reid Wilson, "States Purge Millions of Voters: Report," *THE HILL,* August 1, 2019,

61 Rick Rouan and Doug Caruso, "Ohio's Voter Registration Purge Targeted Thousands in Error. Now, a Call for Change," *The Columbus Dispatch*

Why? Because one conservative voter, Rick Rouan of Ohio, an active voter, was purged in error along with thousands of others. Remember what I said. When the laws impact them, conservatives and Republicans, they change what they do. Just like the poll taxes and literacy tests.

If you think this is illegal, you are sadly mistaken. The US Supreme Court upheld the decision by Georgia to purge people who have not participated in the last three years. The founders giveth, the states taketh away, the Supreme Court approves. Another decision in which justice is blind.

MAIL-IN BALLOTS AND SABOTAGE OF THE POSTAL SYSTEM

Who would have ever thought mail-in ballots and the postal system would be under attack as it relates to voting! People have been using mail-in ballots for years, especially the military personnel who serve overseas. These are normally called absentee ballots. Citizens vote by absentee ballot when they know in advance they will not be able to participate in the election in most states.

States allowed voting by mail for years and as a standard practice, so why is it such an issue now? The legitimacy of our voting process and denouncing intelligence from our experts on Russian involvement has never been questioned.

Now, mail-in ballots are equated to voter fraud. In Oregon's 2016 elections, where over 2 million people voted by mail,

____

and USA TODAY Network, updated January 24, 2020.

only fifty-four cases were proven to be fraud, equating to 0.002 percent. I invite you to watch "Voting by Mail" on *Last Week Tonight with John Oliver* (HBO), who gives a very candid explanation, with cursing, on voting by mail and debunks the lies of Trump.[62]

Our beloved United States Postal Service is near and dear to my heart because my mother was a postal worker. I support them because they move the mail. I pay the little three-dollar charge to get a paper copy because I want to ensure they are employed. I recall being an E-3 on active duty while in basic training in Fort Leonard Wood, Missouri, and how much joy I got during mail call and seeing the faces of others when care packages arrived.

The fact that Louis DeJoy, who is in charge of the post office, started removing mail drop-boxes from many locations is an attempt to disrupt the election. Why would anyone want to slow down the mail now? Ask yourself, why would DeJoy remove postal sorting machines that sort thousands of pieces of mail per minute before a critical election and without a replacement? Not only were the machines removed, but they were also intentionally dismantled, which makes an even stronger statement that the intent is not to return them to the office or have them repaired.

In summary, the aforementioned examples are the most recent methods used in disenfranchising blacks and other minorities at the polls. As I write this book, more things are

---

62 John Oliver, "Voting by Mail." *Last Week Tonight with John Oliver*, HBO, May 31, 2020, YouTube, 19:11.

happening. I have to stop somewhere, yet history and voting are in a constant state of change.

This great country prides itself on the humane treatment of its citizens and deploys its military to war against countries when it sees injustices or when it wants to protect their elections, yet imposes some of the same injustices on its minority citizens. The history of black suppression resulted from the actions of southern states, some individuals, and the failure of *our* government to uphold and exercise its federal powers fairly.

On occasions, Congress failed to fully exercise its powers in the Fourteenth Amendment. It never reduced southern states' congressional representation in proportion to its illegal disenfranchisement, as it was authorized to do. "The Supreme Court actively undermined federal executive powers to protect black voting rights, refused to acknowledge racial discrimination even when it was obvious, and acquiesced in blatant constitutional violations by resorting to specious reasoning."[63]

When you do not exercise your right to vote—state governments know, and they are purging you from the voting rosters. This is yet another way our government seeks ways to get rid of minority voters. The Constitution does not explicitly state if you don't exercise your right to vote, you lose it, so

---

63   J. Morgan Kousser, *The Shaping of Southern Politics: Suffrage Restriction and the Establishment of the One-Party South, 1880-1910* (Yale University Press, 1974); and Samuel Issacharoff, Pamela Karlan, and Richard Pildes, *The Law of Democracy*, (University of Michigan: Foundation Press, 1998).

why are people being purged from the rolls for not voting? Their *why* does not resonate with me and shouldn't with you. Was there an update to the Fifteenth Amendment stating we lose our rights for not exercising our right and I missed it? The Second Amendment, the right to bear arms, is a hot topic. If I decide not to own a weapon, do I lose my right to purchase one because I did not exercise my right to bear arms? Does this make any sense? You know the NRA would be all over this if people's rights were taken away because they decided not to own a weapon. Likewise, we need to be all over the purging of voters for not voting! Purging voters is why blacks feel their vote doesn't matter, but it is also because we are not exercising our right to vote. It is not just about a presidential vote. It is about all elections: presidential, state, and most important, local. Maybe we have not been fully educated, but Chapter Four explains the importance of voting in every single election.

* * *

QUESTION?

Now that you know a bit of the history of additional tactics to block your vote, I ask you the same question Joe Madison asks all of his listeners: What are *you* going to do?

CHAPTER 3

TWO ACTS DON'T MAKE IT RIGHT

Let's face it, when the United States Constitution was drafted, it was not drafted for black people. The Constitution and the laws of this country were not written with us in mind; we just happen to reap the residuals of it via two important acts.

I will admit, in grade school, I had absolutely no interest nor appreciation for history. It was boring to me, and I loathed having to memorize dates about events that meant nothing to me. Not to mention, I hated reading even more. Being made to read and, on top of that, memorize dates of nothing but white history just did not pique my interest. When we did discuss blacks in history, it was routine. Don't get me wrong. The foundation of our history is on the backs of those who came before us and sacrificed their lives, or were Freedom Fighters. The foundation of our history lessons involved discussing Dr. Martin Luther King, Jr., leader of the Civil Rights Movement; Harriet Tubman, famously known for helping slaves escape through the Underground Railroad; and George Washington

Carver, the scientist who came up with so many ways to use the peanut, to name a few.

Unbeknownst to us, there were far too many others we could have studied, such as:

- Ida B. Wells-Barnett (co-founder of the NAACP, anti-lynch crusader, and the most courageous black woman journalist)
- Garrett Morgan (invented the street light)
- Charles R. Drew (invented techniques for preserving blood plasma)
- Madam C.J. Walker (first black female millionaire making hair care products for blacks)
- Benjamin Banneker (self-educated astronomer, mathematician, farmer, author of the farmer's almanacs, surveyor of Washington, DC, and designer of the streets)
- Thomas L. Jennings (first black to hold a patent for dry scouring, which developed into dry cleaning)[64]

Others include:

- Mary Jane McLeod Bethune (educator, founder of a school for black girls known as Bethune College, which merged with Cookman Institute, and is now Bethune-Cookman University)
- Bessie Coleman (first black woman pilot)
- Ida Gray (first black woman in American's history to earn a Doctor of Dental Surgery degree)

---

64 Mary Bellis, "10 Important Black Inventors in U.S. History," *ThoughtCO*, updated January 25, 2019.

- George Washington Bush (an entrepreneur and an early American explorer of the Oregon territory)
- Ebenezer D. Bassett (America's first black diplomat and did so well he became the dean of the American Diplomatic Corps)
- Edward Brooke (elected by the state of Massachusetts' voters to the US Senate in 1966, the first black elected US Senator in America's history, and when blacks accounted for less than 5 percent of the voters)[65]

These are just a few significant blacks in America's history who were never mentioned. Many of them could have been integrated into regular history books, but as I look back, how could they be when the second-hand books blacks received were written for white children and their history. You may ask, "Why didn't you learn about your history from home?" Allow me to give an explanation based on looking back into my own history.

My mother was smart and once worked for the *Columbus Ledger*, a local newspaper company. She married my father, who was in the military, because she was pregnant, and was divorced by the age of thirty with four children.

I was supposed to be a statistic because I grew up in a single-parent home. I was reared by an awesome woman, Rachel Lay Weldon, born during the depression, reared in Fayetteville, North Carolina, divorced, and raising five children. Her main mission was ensuring Maslow's hierarchy of needs

---

65 Empak Enterprises, "Black History" Publication Series, Vols I, III, IX, 1989.

were met—food, safety, love, and self-esteem. By the time I was in the sixth grade, I'd moved six times. My parents divorced while I was in the second grade, and my father gained custody. During my third-grade year, we moved to Panama Canal Zone, where we lived for one year until my father gave custody to my mother in Columbus, Georgia.

At the time, my mother was renting a room when suddenly, there we were. I remained there during my fourth-grade year; mind you, we were living with Aunt Big Gal and Uncle Brugh, the two most unselfish and loving people, who allowed my mother to bring four children into their shotgun home so we would not be on the streets. Thank you, Jesus! Knowing she had to make a way for all of us, she asked my dear, sweet Aunt Jean and Uncle Smitty, who lived in Fayetteville, North Carolina, if my baby brother and I could stay with them until she could get on her feet. They had three children of their own.

Anyway, my aunt and uncle opened their home to us. I lived there for one year, my fifth-grade year, and went home in my sixth-grade year. My mother later got a job with the US Post Office, worked the second shift, cooked dinner before leaving for work, and got home after 11:00 p.m. In my seventh-grade year, my mother had my sister, Kimberly, who is twelve years younger, and whom I practically raised as my own before leaving for the US Army Reserves because my mother now worked the third shift.

As you can deduce, my mother didn't have time to teach us about our history because she was teaching us other things, spoken and unspoken, like making sure our basic needs were met. We were latchkey children, like many others, long before the term existed, but she had rules and we'd better obey them or else. My mother may not have had time to teach us about our history, but she taught us more—respect, work ethic, how to be ladies and gentlemen, strength, and perseverance. These things cannot be taught in a book and seem to be a forgotten responsibility. The history of my people is *my* responsibility, and I must ensure that not only my children are taught, but others as well.

WHAT I LEARNED AT THE FORT VALLEY STATE UNIVERSITY

While attending Fort Valley State College (FVSC), a historical black college and university (HBCU) located in Fort Valley, Georgia, and the only 1890 land-grant university in Georgia, I studied Criminal Justice and fell in love with reading. We read court cases, which definitely piqued my interest, along with having many debates in class. The two instructors who influenced me the most and were instrumental in my interest in reading, justice, and great dialogue were the late Ms. E. Laverne Ford, the first black female warden in the Georgia Department of Corrections, and Attorney Gregory Homer, both graduates of the FVSC, now Fort Valley State University.

They challenged me to dig deeper into legal decisions and encouraged dynamic classroom debates. Since my moral compass was so far north, I did not often agree with some of the outcomes of the cases because I thought they were morally wrong. The instructors welcomed the challenging questions I posed to make me realize it was not about feelings, but the law.

Recently, when I reached out to one former instructor, Mrs. Barbara Palmer, who was trying to help her husband, Dean Palmer, to remember me, said to him, "You know JoJo, Miss Fort Valley, the one with all the mouth." At first, I thought, *Hmm, I'm not quite sure if I should feel some kind of way, but I knew she meant it with love.* I started thinking back to my time on campus and didn't realize I came across as "one with all the mouth"; however, I do recall having conversations about our time in ROTC. A good friend, Elvis Walton, said he wished I had shut up once while in formation because I was going to get everyone in trouble simply because I said what they were thinking.

The awesome Colonel Tyrone Fletcher, Professor of Military Science, who was like a father to all of us, planned for the cadets to go to the Veterans of Foreign Wars (VFW) while conducting tactical training at Fort Benning, Georgia. Instead of going to the VFW, I convinced the cadets to go to the Officer's Club, where the younger crowd partied. The following Monday while in formation, needless to say, Colonel Fletcher was not a happy camper because we were no-shows. Before I knew it, under my breath, I said, "Don't nobody want to go to the VFW where people my mother's age hang out." He asked me what I said. Well, you know me. I repeated it. That didn't go over well either. Elvis reminds me of that day each time we talk, and we have the most gut-wrenching laugh. He told me I always spoke my mind. Ms. Ford and Mr. Homer taught me to speak up, so I guess I am the "one with all the mouth"; thus, here I am today. If something doesn't resonate with me, it is my responsibility to speak up.

Attending the FVSU in the early 1980s opened my eyes to the rich history of my people. Here, like any other HBCU, you *will* learn about the history of *our* black people, *our* contributions to this country, and *our* achievements. You *will* learn to have standards for yourself and others. You *will* be inspired to go places you never dreamed or imagined. You will fall in love with each teacher because you know they care for you and being in the Valley is like being at home. When graduation day comes, you will look back at how far you've come, who you've become, what you've learned, where you are going, and never stop achieving.

This chapter discusses the importance of the Civil Rights Act of 1964, the Voting Rights Act of 1965, and the major impact and shift they had on the history of this country, mainly black people. The Civil and Voting Rights Acts, while passed, I do not feel it was right to have supplements to the Fourteenth and Fifteenth Amendments. And today, neither seem to make a difference—so what will they pass next to ensure we have equal rights and voting rights? I hope you will be inspired to dig deeper into these two acts. Having them doesn't make it right. Start listening for stories in the news about how these acts are being stripped, little by little, yet we don't hear about it until it is too late. The US Army Rangers have a quote that I live by and constantly tell my boys: "Stay Alert, Stay Alive."

THREE IMPORTANT AMENDMENTS TO BLACKS

Let's face it, when The Constitution was drafted, it was not written for black people. The Constitution and the laws of this country were not written with us in mind; we just happen to reap the residuals of it via three important amendments and two acts:

AMENDMENT THIRTEEN: SLAVERY ABOLISHED. RATIFIED 12/6/1865

1. Neither slavery nor involuntary servitude, except as a punishment for crime whereof the party shall have been duly convicted, shall exist within the United States, or any place subject to their jurisdiction.
2. Congress shall have power to enforce this article by appropriate legislation.[66]

AMENDMENT FOURTEEN: CITIZENSHIP RIGHTS. RATIFIED 7/9/1868

3. All persons born or naturalized in the United States, and subject to the jurisdiction thereof, are citizens of the United States and of the state wherein they reside. No state shall make or enforce any law which shall abridge the privileges or immunities of citizens of the United States; nor shall any state deprive any person of life, liberty, or property, without due process of law; nor deny to any person within its jurisdiction the equal protection of the laws…
4. The Congress shall have power to enforce this article by appropriate legislation.[67]

---

66 National Archives, The Constitution of the United States, accessed April 20, 2020.

67 Ibid.

5. The right of citizens of the United States to vote shall not be denied or abridged by the United States or by any state on account of race, color, or previous condition of servitude.

6. The Congress shall have power to enforce this article by appropriate legislation.[68]

BLOCKING BLACK VOTES THROUGH THE UN-JUSTICE SYSTEM

These are the three most important amendments as related to freedom, equal protection, and voting rights in the United States. Let's begin with the Thirteenth Amendment. I have read this one too many times, but recently my son, Donald, a very deep thinker, reminded me of something. While slavery was abolished, this amendment has an "exception to policy," which says, "Slavery nor **involuntary servitude** shall exist within the United States or any place subject to their jurisdiction '**except as a punishment for a crime whereof the party shall have been duly convicted. . . .** '" As Al Sharpton says, "Gotcha." "Servitude is the condition of being a slave or of being completely under the control of someone else."[69] Prison is a form of slavery and a means to strip voting rights.

Kevin Rashid Johnson, a prisoner in Waverly, Virginia, was convicted of murder in 1990 at the age of eighteen, stating it was a case of mistaken identity. He authored an article in *The Guardian* titled "Prison Labor Is Modern Slavery. I've

---

68 Ibid.

69 *Collins Dictionary*, s.v. "servitude," accessed April 20, 2020,

Been Sent to Solitary for Speaking Out," attesting to the last statement in the Thirteenth Amendment that "under the Thirteenth Amendment slavery was not abolished, it was merely reformed." Prisoners are chained together, placed in fields where they grow the crops they eat, and use primitive tools to dig up the land and plant cotton. Also, guards ride horses doing constant patrol, using coercion and violence to keep prisoners in line.[70]

When he became rebellious and spoke out about the treatment by boycotting the commissary, not eating or working under the awful conditions, they put him on death row, but he was not a death row prisoner. The intent was to ensure he was so isolated that he could not influence other inmates. He was amazed that under such isolation, he was able to get his article in *The Guardian*.[71]

Examine that last part of the first line entered in the Thirteenth Amendment. It was put there by design. Are you reading with a third eye? Yes, they put it in writing that blacks could vote, but they also put in writing how to put blacks back in a system of slavery. Prison, then and now, is a double-edged sword, because until recently, not only are blacks put back into an institution of slavery, but blacks also lose their right to vote. "As of 2018, Mr. Johnson pointed out that Virginia's general population of African Americans is

---

70   Kevin Rashid Johnson, "Opinion U.S. Prison, Prison Labor Is Modern Slavery. I've Been Sent to Solitary for Speaking Out," *The Guardian*, August 23, 2018.

71   Ibid.

19 percent, but 58 percent of its prison population is black."[72] If you really think about it, our government removed blacks from the streets of freedom to purge them from the voting rolls long before. I still say legal laws were passed that should have been illegal, purging nonvoters for exercising their right *not* to vote. Like everything else, why can't *not voting* be a form of free speech? Because the laws apply based on who is impacted.

Whenever blacks are imprisoned, they are, in essence, thrown back into a form of slavery. Granted, some deserve to be there, no doubt, but others are jailed for not committing a crime, being coerced into saying they did, or being poor and not being able to afford a lawyer to work on their behalf to get them out. Blacks are targeted, in most cases, just for being black. Here are some known examples of why blacks are jailed more than whites:

- Police practice discrimination and racial profiling.
- Driving while black.
- Black children in school systems receive harsher punishments than whites for the same offense, in which some schools call the police.
- When white children are caught by police, in most cases, they are released to their parents while black children are placed in the juvenile system.
- Blacks cannot afford bail, which is often set too high.
- Blacks go to jail for small amounts of marijuana, which is now legal, or drugs introduced into the black communities in the 1970s and 1980s, while whites don't go to jail

---

72 Ibid.

for more potent drugs or now opioids. Instead, the government budgets for opioid treatment and classifies this as an illness. Some states even set up treatment facilities.

- Blacks plead guilty more because they cannot afford a good lawyer, are beaten or coerced into saying they did the crime when they are in fact not guilty, or end up in prison on trumped-up charges.
- Blacks are repeat offenders when they get out if they cannot find a job because, let's face it, who wants to take a chance on a person with a criminal history, even if it is minor or a false arrest?
- Blacks are arrested more than whites simply for being black, and the prison system, especially when privatized, is a big money-making business requiring it to be filled at a certain capacity.

These examples are known to black people, and much of this is outlined by Mr. Bill Quigley's, Law Professor at Loyola University in New Orleans, study: "Why Jails Are Full of Black And Poor People."[73] Although the crime rate decreased under President Obama, these reasons for incarcerating blacks and the poor still exist. Beyond going to prison, blacks are being killed daily by one another, but more so by the very people who are supposed to protect us, and for no reason. Some police tend to shoot first and lie to cover it up, but thank God for cell phones to provide actual footage. Some police officers are the judge, jury, and executioner without due process.

---

73 Bill Quigley, "40 Reasons Why Our Jails Are Full of Black and Poor People," *HuffPost*, dated June 2, 2015.

JIM CROW LAWS AND SEPARATE BUT EQUAL

The Fourteenth Amendment is where things go awry. This amendment states if I am born on the soil of the United States, I have the same rights and privileges as a white person. News flash! This was a lie then and holds true today, for the most part. *If* blacks, who were born in these United States of America are citizens; *If* no state shall deprive any person of life, liberty, or property, without due process of law; nor deny to any person within its jurisdiction the equal protection of the laws . . . and *if* Congress shall have the power to enforce this article by appropriate legislation, then why, one hundred fifty plus years later, are blacks still fighting for equal protection of the law? Why did President Kennedy propose the Civil Rights Act before his assassination, and President Lyndon B. Johnson asked Congress to pass it in memory of President Kennedy? Why? Because blacks did not have equal rights under the Fourteenth Amendment as written.

After Reconstruction, southern whites regained political control and implemented laws to segregate blacks and whites. Why? Because blacks left the farm life where sharecropping was a moneymaker and business for the white Southerners and moved to southern cities. With no one to work the farms, and blacks seeming to be thriving on their own, southern whites implemented a new racial order nicknamed the "Jim Crow" era. "This era made racial lines on what blacks could and could not do and where they could and could not live. This is when separate neighborhoods came into existence;

separate water fountains, bathrooms, train cars, etc., all known as 'separate but equal.'"[74]

PLESSY V. FERGUSON

The Civil Rights movement challenged Jim Crow laws starting with Plessy v. Ferguson, when Plessy, who was mixed with white blood, challenged Louisiana's Separate Car Act. He contended that since he was seven-eighths white, he should be able to sit in the "whites-only" car.[75] This caused another challenge for the courts because now the question of "one-drop" rule came into play. The "one-drop" rule of the nineteenth century meant if any white person had "one-drop" of black blood, they were black. With that being said, the Supreme Court upheld the Louisiana law stating it was not unconstitutional as long as blacks and whites had the same facility, equal but separate, then there was no violation of the Jim Crow laws.[76] Face it, the Jim Crow Law was illegal and the Supreme Court was blind to the actual laws of the Constitution. Remember, laws are passed based on who they impact.

BROWN V. BOARD OF EDUCATION

Another case challenging Jim Crow laws was Brown v. Board of Education of Topeka, in which Thurgood Marshall argued

---

74 Lisa Vox, "The Civil Rights Act of 1964 Did Not End the Movement For Equality," *ThoughtCo*, updated February 14, 2019.

75 Cornell Law School, Legal Information Institute, "Plessy v. Ferguson," Supreme Court, accessed September 20, 2020.

76 Don Jaide, "Plessy v. Ferguson: The Meaning of the 'One-Drop" Rule,' *Africare Source*, November 20, 2011.

separate facilities were not equal. As blacks began to take a stand against the injustice of the Jim Crow laws, next came the Montgomery bus boycott, sit-ins of 1960, and Freedom Rides of 1961. The first paragraph of the act states that its purpose is "to enforce the constitutional right to vote, to confer jurisdiction . . . relief against discrimination in public accommodations . . . institute suits to protect . . . public education . . . prevent discrimination in federally assisted programs . . . Commission on Equal Employment Opportunity." [77]

CIVIL RIGHTS ACT OF 1964

President Lyndon B. Johnson signed the Civil Rights Act into law on July 2, 1964. It was supposed to guarantee an end to segregation and discrimination regarding schools, public places and activities, and employment.[78] Again, I pose the question: If we are citizens of these United States of America, why did we need a supplement to the Fourteenth Amendment? Allow me to tell you why. I reiterate, we *never* had the same rights as whites, no matter how much we did what they said we needed to do, such as work hard, educate ourselves, pull yourself up by your bootstraps, or learn the culture of the white man to become self-sufficient. When a race feels they own you for life, it is hard to escape the evils of their deeds.

---

77 Lisa Vox, "The Civil Rights Act of 1964 Did Not End the Movement For Equality," *ThoughtCo*, updated February 14, 2019.

78 GovInfo, "The Civil Rights Act of 1964, 78 Stat. 241 - Civil Rights Act - July 2, 1964," accessed April 21, 2020,

In 1963, more than approximately 344 years after slaves were brought to Virginia, and approximately ninety-five years after the ratification of the Fourteenth Amendment, blacks were still treated like trash, with an unspoken rule that we better "stay in our place" or reap the consequences. Some whites today still feel we are not deserving of the same rights as them simply because of the color of our skin. Again, I ask, why do they hate us?

THE VOTING RIGHTS ACT OF 1965

President Johnson also signed the Voting Rights Act into law on August 6, 1965. It "aimed to overcome legal barriers at the state and local levels which prevented blacks from exercising our right to vote under the Fifteenth Amendment."[79] Why did blacks need Dr. Martin Luther King, Jr. and others to fight so hard to get the Voting Rights Act of 1965 passed to get what we had as a right by birth? I asked this question of Mrs. Willa Lewis, my second mother, and she explained it like this. When America saw the events unfold on the Edmund Pettus Bridge in Selma, Alabama, known as Bloody Sunday, live on television of the senseless beatings of blacks by the very people who were supposed to protect us, it tugged at the hearts of Americans. They had to do something!

PURGING NONVOTERS

Remember, I felt the need to write this book after hearing on the radio Georgia was purging voters. I drove home with a

---

79 The Editors of Encyclopaedia Britannica, "The Voting Rights Act," *Britannica,* last updated July 20, 2020.

purpose to do my research to find out how. Research showing the Supreme Court sided with Georgia's law angered me. This one bothers me the most. Where in the Fifteenth Amendment does it state if you do not vote, you lose your right? How can a state make a law more restrictive to an amendment in the Constitution? Let's revisit this one again: "The right of citizens of the United States to vote shall not be denied or abridged by the United States or by any state on account of race, color, or previous condition of servitude. Congress shall have the power to enforce this article by appropriate legislation." Congress is not enforcing a damn thing to protect the rights of voters, nor is the Supreme Court.

Stripping voters from the voting registry is yet another effort to hinder voters from exercising their right, as with the state of Texas, when David Whitley, Texas' Secretary of State, led efforts to find noncitizens on the state's voter rolls. When a question of citizenship came up, a federal judge stopped the state's effort to purge voter rolls, because approximately ninety thousand voters in 2019 were affected. After several lawsuits, the citizens were reinstated.[80]

The state of Ohio is also purging voters from the rolls for not voting and the Supreme Court upheld it. Ohio election officials state they send a notice to every voter who didn't vote in a two-year period. If they don't respond, and don't vote over the next four years, which includes two additional federal elections, they are dropped from the registry. So, if you have not voted in a six-year period, you are dropped. "A.

---

80 Amy Lopez, "Texas Voting Chief Who Led Botched Voter Purge Resigns," National Public Radio, WAMU 88.5, May 28, 2019.

Philip Randolph Institute said it violated the National Voter Registration Act, which specifies that voters can be purged from the rolls only if they ask, move, are convicted of a felony, become mentally incapacitated, or die."[81]

In summary, as you can see, passing these two acts "don't make it right." The Civil Rights Act of 1964 was passed to ensure the rights of the Fourteenth Amendment were implemented for blacks. The Voting Rights Act of 1965 was passed to ensure the rights of the Fifteenth Amendment were implemented, too. While the intent was good, it was not right that blacks needed a "supplement" to these amendments to get what was rightfully ours, the right to live in this country with everyone else, and with equal rights free from harassment, discrimination, and the right to vote. Just because these two acts were passed does not make it right and doesn't seem to help in some instances. No other race has additional laws implemented to have rights guaranteed under the Constitution—It Still Ain't Right.

* * *

QUESTION:

What are you going to do to ensure the Jim Crow laws of the past stay in the past?

---

81   Pete Williams, "Supreme Court Gives Ohio Right to Purge Thousands of Voters from Its Rolls," NBC News, June 11, 2018.

CHAPTER 4

ALL ELECTIONS ARE IMPORTANT

If the Senate confirms another conservative to the Supreme Court, the list of accomplishments Justice Ginsburg fought for will surely be reversed. She fought for equal rights for everyone, regardless of skin color or sexual orientation, to include women's rights and equal pay.

Shortly after graduating from the FVSC, now FVSU, I was stationed at Fort Hood, Texas, Second Armored Division. I recall having a discussion about being taxed by the county for something dealing with the school system. I didn't have any children, so why was I paying these taxes? I, along with many young people, with or without children, are taxed on things you *feel* you should not be taxed on.

Why should I, now an empty nester, pay for any taxes relevant to the school system in my county? The answer is simple: I live here; therefore, my tax dollars support the county schools. The property taxes help pay for numerous things in each county, including teachers' salaries. Why should I pay an additional tax at the grocery store for the Metro's Purple Line being built going to Dulles International Airport when I don't even fly out of Dulles International Airport? Because this project must be funded, I live in the state of Virginia, and a law was passed requiring all residents to pay these taxes. Your zip code really does determine the amount of taxes you pay. The more taxes one pays, the better the school systems.

Many of you understand you are going to pay taxes—point blank. However, do you know where and how your tax dollars are applied? Most likely not. Check with your local county and/or municipality to find out the additional taxes you are paying and why. For example, it was not until I looked at my monthly mortgage statement that I discovered I was paying a fee to the county fire department. The state legislature decided I was going to pay this fee and I don't mind.

This was also great information to know because I often received calls from the police department with an area code 757, soliciting donations for this cause or that cause and promising to send me tickets to an event I am sure I would never attend. Then, a couple of years later, I learned my county's police never solicit money from the public by asking for donations. So, the next time I received a call, I played with them for a bit and then let them know they were scammers. Besides, why would I donate to an area code three hours away?

You may be wondering why I am bringing these issues up and how they relate to voting. It relates to voting in that decisions affecting our community are made at the local and state levels, and many blacks have no clue because we, for the most part as a race, do not attend county meetings. Another reason we don't have a clue is that we are not looking at the news, reading the news, or listening to any informative substance to become more informed. I'm sorry, Facebook is not a news feed.

This chapter focuses on educating why all elections are important, and how the local and state elections impact your daily life. They have the most direct impact on our community while the presidential election impacts the nation as a whole. This chapter also explains how the Office of the President impacts us for decades.

LOCAL ELECTIONS

Local elections, like all elections, allow citizens to vote someone into an office who they feel has their best interest at heart and, in most cases, is someone at the grassroots level. It may be a pastor who is running for office for his or her district, or someone you grew up with who feels he or she can make a difference in the city or town where they reside. Regardless of the position, they serve on that particular local council. They are responsible for "making general policies, passing laws, supervising the city government, and appropriating funds for various needs." According to the National League of Cities, located in Washington, DC, here is a list of the city council's responsibilities:

- Review and approve the annual budget
- Establish long- and short-term objectives and priorities
- Oversee performance of the local public employees

- Oversee effectiveness of programs
- Establish tax rates
- Enter into legal contracts
- Borrow funds
- Pass ordinances and resolutions
- Modify the city's charter
- Regulate land use through zoning laws
- Regulate business activity through licensing and regulations
- Regulate public health and safety
- Exercise the power of eminent domain
- Communicate policies and programs to residents
- Respond to constituent needs and complaints
- Represent the community to other levels of government[82]

Now that you have an idea of these responsibilities, you can learn how each item affects you directly. Let's look at just a few, such as reviewing and approving the annual budget. We need to ensure our city council member is providing information about how and where your taxes are applied. If not, google it (Google is your friend). Another reason we need to know how our money is applied is because as of September 20, 2020, the US national debt is over 26 trillion dollars and rising.[83] This clock also allows you to see the world's debt and your state's debt. As of October 18, 2020, 3:25 p.m., the national debt was over **27 trillion dollars**, while the state of Virginia had a debt over **67 billion dollars.** Since trillions of dollars are currently being spent due to COVID-19, the

---

82 National League of Cities, "City Council," accessed September 20, 2020.

83 U.S. Debt Clock, accessed October 18, 2020.

states have to look at the budget to figure out how to get the revenue to operate the state.

For the Fiscal Year 2021, the tax levy on real estate in Prince William County will be 1.125 dollars per 100 dollars of the assessed value. Recall when I mentioned I learned if I paid taxes for the fire department? Well, the tax levy for each real estate property will be 0.080 dollars per 100 dollars assessed value of your home for fire and rescue purposes.[84]

It would behoove each of you to do your own research to find out how your county, town, city, or municipality is currently and will start taxing its citizens to get the revenue needed to operate. It is impossible for a person to run for office and say they will not raise taxes, because taxing the citizens is how a city earns its operating budget to support infrastructure improvements, snow removal, parks, etcetera.

Another important responsibility of our city council, besides exercising the power of eminent domain (which is when the government can take possession of your property when they feel they need to for the greater good of the city), is to respond to needs and complaints from its constituents—that's us! When we do not participate in the local meetings, vote in elections where issues are put on the ballot, refuse to read the ballots, or skip these issues, how can the council member hear from their constituents? One thing for sure, they cannot read our minds. To them, no complaints means they are doing a satisfactory job, and if this is not the case,

---

84 Prince William County Government, "Virginia Government e-documents," accessed August 4, 2020.

we are the problem for not doing our job as a hardworking tax-paying citizen.

As I write this and watch CNN, my heart has been heavy all week by the protests all over America for the killing of Mr. George Floyd, an unarmed black man, by a white police officer, Derek Chauvin. With his hands in his pockets, he appeared to take great pleasure in forcing his knee on Mr. Floyd's neck. Mr. Floyd was accused of attempting to purchase something with a fake twenty-dollar bill. He was on the ground, handcuffed, legs held down by two other police officers, and face pressed on the curb. Blacks are outraged! This time, white, brown, and many other races are just as outraged! This officer had eighteen complaints against him. It took four days to arrest him even with video coverage showing his actions whereas blacks are often arrested and killed without any evidence by an officer who acts as judge, jury, and executioner.

Senseless killings is one of the reasons the black community feels our vote doesn't matter, but it is also because we are not exercising all our rights in voting. How can our vote matter if we are not voting? It is not just about a presidential vote. Don't get me wrong, that election is so very important in other ways, but the issues impacting our day-to-day lives start at the local level. We have a voice in how the police treat us when we vote and participate in the local meetings. All elections are important: presidential, state, and, most importantly, local.

STATE ELECTIONS

When I was growing up, my brothers, sister, and I crowded in front of one television to watch the Saturday cartoons, only after we completed our chores. I remember after each cartoon went off, one of the educational entertainment segments was *Schoolhouse Rock!* They were awesome. The one that comes to mind as I write this section was titled "I'm Just a Bill." It teaches how an idea from constituents (remember, that's you) is presented to their congressman, who introduces it to Congress, where it becomes a bill. It is discussed and debated in committee, then voted on in the House of Representatives. If they vote yes, it goes to the Senate Chamber. If they vote yes, then it goes to the president's desk, who has the power to veto it, but if he doesn't, and signs it, it then becomes law.[85] It's really cute with a great song, too.

Here is a little bit of history. Congress is composed of two chambers. The first one is the House of Representatives, often referred to as the House. It has four hundred thirty-five voting members and six nonvoting members in case of vacancies. They serve a two-year term, meaning every two years we should be voting for our state's representative who represents our district. The number of representatives for each state is based on the population from the United States Census. So, this means, every election year and midterm, we need to be standing in a line, no matter how long, to vote for the ones who represent our values.[86]

---

85 Schoolhouse Rock, "I'm Just a Bill," YouTube, 3:00.

86 Congressman Langevin, Jim, "Understanding Congress," accessed October 1, 2020.

The second chamber is the Senate, with one hundred voting members, two per state, no matter the population. They serve a six-year term, meaning every two years, approximately one-third of these seats are up for election. So, let's do the math. Every two years, we need to exercise our voting rights for the people who will make a significant difference in our state.[87]

The *Schoolhouse Rock!* video teaches that both chambers have equal powers in the legislative process, meaning both determine if an idea becomes a bill and present it to the president to sign into law. When President Obama was elected in 2008 and took office in 2009, he was able to get his legislative agenda through because both chambers were controlled by the Democrats. From 2015 to 2017, the Senate flipped to majority Republican, resulting in Senate Majority Leader Mitch McConnell blocking the president's ability to confirm Merrick Garland. The Republicans also ensured President Obama's agenda hit a brick wall, with everything he attempted to do.[88] Bottom line, as previously stated, your representatives to Congress are the ones who push the constituents' wishes through to get laws passed. Your state's representatives are the *real* ones making decisions impacting you for years.

CONGRESSIONAL VOTES DATABASE

Another thing you should start doing, if you currently do not, is google how your representative votes. Visit the

---

87   Ibid.

88   Susan Davis, "Senate Republicans Agree To Block Obama's Supreme Court Nominee," NPR, February 23, 2016.

Congressional Votes Database to track how your state's representatives voted on different issues.[89] During the campaign period, our representatives have a platform they want us to buy into. If they tell us they will fight for us, we believe it, but how do we really know if they have our best interest at heart? We don't. That is why we need to do our homework by researching how they vote on issues affecting us. If you ever saw *The West Wing*, you will understand "drug deals" are made between Congressional members to persuade one Congress member to vote for a bill and vice versa. The one thing we hope is the person we elect to represent our state and our wishes votes in favor of bills that not only benefit us but all humanity.

Lastly, at the state level is the election for governor, known as the gubernatorial elections. This position is voted on by the constituents (us). Virginia Governor Terry McAuliffe, in April 2016, restored voting rights for approximately two hundred thousand felons who paid their debts to society, which included fines, supervised probation, or parole. His compassion for this initiative was even more because he also told them he wanted them to have full rights as a citizen, working, paying taxes, and no longer considered second-class citizens.[90] These words were then and are still powerful.

Governor Terry McAuliffe understood one in four blacks were imprisoned and the laws in Virginia did not grant

---

89 Govtracks, "Voting Records," Congressional Votes Database, accessed September 22, 2020.

90 Doug Mataconis, "Virginia Governor Restores Voting Rights to 200,000 Ex-Felons," Outside the Beltway, April 23, 2016.

voting rights to felons. He signed an executive order eliminating the need for felons to complete an application to have their rights reinstated. This order removed the arduous process of getting reinstated, causing felons to give up. Virginia Republican House Speaker William J. Howell of Stafford County criticized this move.[91] The big question is why didn't he want their rights restored? They did the time, paid fines, and completed supervised parole, so based on the Fifteenth Amendment, this right shall not be denied based on a previous condition of servitude. This is a prime example of electing someone into office whose platform supports your views for the greater good of humanity. If the Bible says we should forgive a man seventy times seven for his sins, why can't a felon be given a second chance once paying his debt? (Matthew 18:22, KJV)

PRESIDENTIAL ELECTION

The Office of President is the highest in the United States, and the world, for that matter, and should be occupied by the best candidate. This person is responsible for all fifty states and territories, for he or she, too, is elected by the people, though not by the popular or majority vote because there is that thing called the Electoral College. The Electoral College is simply a number of electors (everyday people) in each state based on the total number of representatives and senators. They make a significant difference in the presidential election. When a candidate wins the popular vote for that state, they receive the number of Electoral College votes representative of that state and its population. A candidate

---

91   Ibid.

must win two hundred seventy Electoral College votes to win the presidency.[92]

So, your candidate wins the election and becomes President of the United States. Yay! In order for your newly elected president to make the changes promised during the campaign, you must also vote the party line. Why? Because if your party in Congress (House of Representatives and Senate) does not match the party of the president, he or she will have a difficult time getting any laws passed that you voted for, for the greater good of the country. If you did not vote party line during the election and in the midterm elections, you may as well have not voted in the Presidential one. Remember in a previous paragraph, President Obama had a difficult time getting his agenda through because the Republicans were the majority and blocked all his initiatives, even blocking him from selecting a Supreme Court Judge. To get the president's agenda through, we must vote the party line.

OFFICE OF THE PRESIDENT AND ITS POWERS

The Office of the President has many powers that impact the world and our daily lives. Did you know one of the powers the office has is the right to appoint judges at the Circuit Court, Federal Court, and Supreme Courts? In four years, President Trump appointed 198 judges who will sit on the bench for the rest of their lives, and not one is black. He appointed two to the Supreme Court, fifty-plus to the appellate courts,

---

92 History.com Editors, "Electoral College," History, updated September 27, 2019, Original January 12, 2010.

and the rest to district courts, who will sit in that position for the rest of their lives.

Why is this important? "Voting is not about the next four years but the next forty years." In a sermon titled "Birth of a Nation, Part 2," Reverend Dr. Howard-John Wesley, who provided the data in the previous paragraph, also made this profound statement: "When you don't vote, not only are you disrespecting our past, but jeopardizing the future of justice in this land."[93]

I hope you listen to his words. "If you don't vote, you are not casting your voice about the district and state attorneys in your local communities. Justice begins with the district attorneys, who make decisions about who goes to trial, organizes plea bargains, or fails to indict officers for killing black people. When you don't vote, you have no say in the person who goes to trial or who walks without indictment. You are not eligible to serve in the jury of peers and advocate for someone who looks like you for lesser sentencing or equal justice under the law."[94]

This sermon is so powerful, and I thought to myself, *Is he in my head?* I stated earlier that when we do not vote, we are disenfranchising our community, too. Please listen to the sermon for I promise you it is so well worth it. I learned something and know you will, too.

---

93 "Reverend Dr. Howard John Wesley Pastor, "Birth of a Nation, Part 2," Alfred Street Baptist Church, Alexandria, Virginia, July 14, 2020, YouTube. 44:41.

94 Ibid.

SUPREME COURT JUSTICES

Today is Tuesday, September 22, 2020, and the most powerful Think Tank of the Supreme Court, Justice Ruth Bader Ginsburg, known as the Notorious RBG, died this past Saturday. What a devastating blow to this country! She was a powerhouse, quiet and classy. She and conservative Justice Antonin Scalia were very good friends, but she was like E.F. Hutton: When she spoke, everyone listened. Justice RBG was a liberal supreme court justice appointed by President Bill Clinton on June 4, 1993.

Justice Ginsburg is notable for the following:

- Fought for gender equality
- Fought against sexism
- Fought for equal pay under the passage of the Lilly Ledbetter Fair Pay Act
- Fought for women's rights and rejected Roe v. Wade
- Co-founded the Women's Rights Project at ACLU
- Won five of six cases argued before the Supreme Court
- First Justice to officiate a same-sex marriage
- Fought for widowers to get social security benefits[95]

Before Justice Ginsburg passed, the makeup of the Supreme Court was five conservatives and four liberal justices. This made the playing field a little bit better in that perhaps Justice Ginsburg could win the heart of at least one to see things her way. In less than thirty minutes before her eyes were closed, McConnell could not wait to announce filling her seat before

---

95   Mathew Blake, "42 Factinate, Notorious Big, Powerful Facts about Ruth Bader Ginsburg," Factinate, accessed October 3, 2020.

the next election. Mind you, when President Obama was in office, they blocked him from filling a vacancy, stating the "people should pick the next justice." My, how the tables turn.

If the Senate confirms another conservative, the list of accomplishments Justice Ginsburg fought for will surely be reversed. She fought for equal rights for everyone, regardless of skin color or sexual orientation, to include women's rights and equal pay, to name a few. The Supreme Court will consist of six conservatives and three liberals, the ones fighting for the little people, like us, will not stand a chance, and all the progress made in this country will be reversed. As I write this section, the Affordable Care Act is in front of the Supreme Court to repeal. Along with coverage for preexisting diseases—millions of Americans will lose health care, all because you decided your vote was not worth your time!

After all, how can the government make decisions about a woman's body? Amazing how people are protesting about their right not to wear a mask, free speech, and the government cannot tell them what to do, and their voices are heard. When it comes to Roe v. Wade, the government has control over a woman's right to control her body. How can the government claim to care about the unborn when a woman decides to have an abortion, but have not an issue with over 210 thousand people dead from COVID-19? How can the government claim to care about killing unborn children, but not care about the five-hundred-plus living immigrant children in cages who were ripped from their parents and now cannot find their parents? How can the government claim to care about life, but care less about the death of innocent blacks? Here is my thought on Roe v. Wade: For every sin every man or woman commits, they will have to answer to God, not man. One sin is not worse than the other—for sin is sin!

Last but not least, when considering who you want as the leader of these United States, I implore you to vote for someone who is qualified, not someone who you think is going to be a savior. We have only one savior who died for our sins. I don't care who you vote for, but by all means, vote for someone whose agenda aligns with what you want to see done for this country.

Your job is to look at the records of each candidate. This may require you to actually put it down on paper and not do this in your head. Weigh the pros and cons of each candidate; figure out what you absolutely cannot live with between them; and whichever one has the most pros, select that one. If not, you will surely regret your vote, and you will be an irresponsible voter. Let me make this perfectly clear: there will never be a perfect candidate and we are not perfect people, but we must make the best-educated decision or we will surely suffer for it for years, and there *ain't* a damn thing you can complain about if you didn't vote.

In summary, I tried to give a brief explanation of why all elections are important from the local, to the state, to the presidential. The elections that impact what is happening in your backyard are the most important because they affect your everyday life, from your children's teachers, curriculum, and local taxes, to police reform in the midst of the murder of George Floyd and other black men videoed being killed while in police custody. Ensuring the right candidates are in your city council makes a huge difference in getting legislation changed when they hear from their constituents (remember, that is *you*).

Unfortunately, Mr. Floyd's death captured the entire world's attention. It showed how dangerous it is to be a black man confronted by police. When black citizens are in the custody of some police officers, they lose their lives unnecessarily, and without any repercussions. This has to stop! There must be some type of reform to ensure there are consequences for killing anyone simply because you wear a badge. Change happens when you change your mindset and realize there is power in your vote. Why else did the Virginia Republicans have a problem with felons voting? What other reason is there for states purging people from the rolls for not exercising their right to free speech by not voting? I will tell you why. It's simple—because they know you don't vote. When you decide not to vote, your right to vote is slipping away with each election.

* * *

QUESTION:
What does voting mean to you? Which of Justice Ginsburg's legislative works would you hate to lose? What will you do to ensure this country does not slip back to the time when equal rights were not so equal?

PART 2

ISSUES AFFECTING BLACK COMMUNITIES

CHAPTER 5

EDUCATION: AN IMPORTANT ISSUE TO BLACKS

———

When books are written to specifically overlook the contributions of not just the black race, but any race, this is a prime example of "whitewashing," which is an attempt to stop people finding out the true facts about a situation.

In my introduction, I discussed the reason we did not learn the depth of black history growing up, because the white authors didn't write the history books for us. They were written specifically for the white race. Oh, they knew our history, but it was not important to them. When books are written to specifically overlook the contributions of not just the black race, but any race, this is a prime example of "whitewashing," which is an attempt to stop people from finding out the true facts about a situation.[96]

You'd have to ask yourself, why is the true history of this country omitted? Is it because the whites didn't give a damn about the black race and our history? Is it because if we knew our history, we would want more? Or is it because if the world knew how hateful and mean-spirited whites were toward blacks, all while living under the auspice of being *Christians*, this would shatter their image? Perhaps it's all of them.

My mother hated Columbus Day. She always said, "How can America say Columbus discovered it when it wasn't lost? The Native Americans were here first."

Native Americans were robbed of their land. In essence, America's land, occupied by Native Americans, was raped and pillaged, too, after they tried to be helpful to teach the white men about the land and crops. Now America celebrates *Thanksgiving*. I recently learned a friend's husband does not celebrate Thanksgiving because it is based on a pure lie. Think about this question for a moment: Is America celebrating or thankful for stealing the land, pretending to be friendly, raping and killing Native Americans, and isolating them to reservations (and they, too, should just be satisfied)? Think back to the old western movies and television shows. For the most part, the Native Americans were cast as the enemy. Ask yourself, who was the real enemy?

---

96 Cambridge Dictionary, s.v. "whitewashing (n.)," accessed September 23, 2020.

Today is Juneteenth, June 19, a day I take leave from my job to celebrate my people's freedom from slavery, even if America doesn't observe it. I have been doing this for a few years. I learned of Juneteenth many years ago and thought to myself, well damn. Then I said, "Self, you need to start taking that day off. That is your Fourth of July, and a day for you to celebrate it, because America sure isn't."

Let's discuss a few pieces of history you most likely will never see in the history books. Remember, the history books were then, and still are today, written for white America.

JUNETEENTH

Let me start by saying slavery was all over the world. Africans were transported throughout the world and sold, with West Africa being the biggest slave port. They were kidnapped and sold by many different countries, such as Benin, which sold slaves to the Portuguese, French, and British merchants en route to Brazil, Haiti, and the US.[97] Let this sink in. We were human trafficked long before the term was introduced.

Abraham Lincoln issued a preliminary Emancipation Proclamation on September 22, 1862, declaring as of January 1, 1863, all slaves in the states rebelling against the Union "shall be then, henceforward, and forever free."[98] The Thirteenth Amendment was passed by Congress on January 31, 1865,

---

97 Kevin Dieff, "An African Country Reckons with Its History of Selling Slaves," Washington Post, January 29, 2018.

98 Terry Tang, "APExplains: Juneteenth Marks Days Last Enslaved People Free," APNews, June 18, 2020.

ratified December 8, 1865, (eight months after the end of the Civil War) and declared in a proclamation of the Secretary of State on December 18, 1865, to have been ratified by twenty-seven of thirty-six states.[99] Texas did not ratify the amendment until February 18, 1870.

While researching the US Constitution, I learned Delaware did not ratify until February 12, 1901, and believe it or not, Kentucky ratified on March 18, 1976.[100] I am thinking to myself, this must be a misprint! What was even more shocking is, as of 1976, Mississippi had yet to ratify the Thirteenth Amendment.

This prompted me to google when Mississippi ratified the Thirteenth Amendment. I found that Mississippi finally voted to ratify the Thirteenth Amendment in 1995 but failed to make it official by notifying the US Archivist. Dr. Ranjan Batra, an Indian professor of Neurobiology and Anatomical Sciences at the University of Mississippi Medical Center, learned this while conducting deeper research into Mississippi after watching a film titled *Lincoln*. He then contacted Dr. Ken Sullivan, a black colleague of the University of Mississippi Medical Center, who contacted Mississippi's Secretary of State, Delbert Hosemann, of the oversight. Then on January 30, 1995, Hosemann sent the Office of the Federal

---

99 National Constitution Center, Interactive Constitution, "13th Amendment, Abolition of Slavery," accessed June 6, 2020.

100 The Constitution of the United States, Bill of Rights and All Amendments, "13th Amendment," accessed June 6, 2020.

Register a copy of the 1995 resolution. The ratification was official February 7, 1995. I must say, this is a shame![101]

Back to Juneteenth. Slaves in Texas did not find out about the Emancipation Proclamation until Major General Gordon Granger arrived in Galveston and informed the state all slaves were free on June 19, 1965.[102] This prompted the celebration of *Juneteenth*. As you can see, all states did not ratify within a year or two. It took many years for a few states to get on board with slaves being free.

BLACK WALL STREET

Another black moment in history not found in the history books is Tulsa's Black Wall Street. Some freed slaves migrated from the South to eastern Oklahoma, formerly Indian territory, to make a way of life after slavery. While in Tulsa, blacks flourished as business owners from 1865 to 1920. Greenwood was named after a city in Mississippi by O.W. Gurley, a wealthy black landowner who purchased forty acres of land in Tulsa. This part of Tulsa was a wealthy self-contained community of affluent black business owners with "restaurants, luxury shops, grocery stores, hotels, jewelry and clothing stores, movie theaters, barbershops and

---

101 Ken Sullivan, "Throwback Thursday: Mississippi & The Thirteenth Amendment 2013," updated February 16, 2020.

102 Henry Lewis Gates, Jr., "What is Juneteenth," originally posted on The Root (blog), PBS, African Americans: Many Rivers to Cross, accessed June 25, 2020.

salons, library, pool halls, nightclubs, and offices for doctors, lawyers, and dentists."[103]

Naturally, this gained the attention of jealous whites who thought blacks were inferior to them and did not deserve what they accomplished. I imagine they were thinking, too, how in the world did they do this, or get this, and it is equal to or better than what I own.

In 1921, Sharon Page, a seventeen-year-old white elevator operator, accused a nineteen-year-old black shoe shiner, Dick Rowland, of assault, but the Tulsa Tribune printed a story the next day changing the assault to attempted rape.

Later that night, mobs of blacks and whites appeared at the jail where Dick was held. An armed black man, who was there to protect Dick, shot a white protestor during a confrontation, thus starting the Tulsa massacre. Approximately three hundred blacks died over a two-day period and were placed in mass graves or dumped into the Arkansas River, and greater than nine hundred found themselves homeless after Greenwood burned to the ground.[104]

During the days of racial tension toward black men, white women had an MO (*modus operandi,* meaning an individual's or group's habitual way of operating, which forms a

---

103 Alexis Clark, "Tulsa's 'Black Wall Street' Flourished as a Self-Contained Hub in Early 1900s," History, updated January 2, 2020.

104 Alexis Clark, "Tulsa's 'Black Wall Street' Flourished as a Self-Contained Hub in Early 1900s," History, updated January 2, 2020.

discernible pattern).[105] They have a history of blaming black men for things they did not do, especially rape or sexual assault, knowing full well this would result in a killing by a weapon, a severe beating, or lynching. It did not stop there. It occurred throughout the United States—the same country where white men claim to be Christians and Lady Justice is blind—only blind to white crime.

BECKYS AND KARENS OF THE PAST

Let me pause for a moment to say all white women were not this way, but there are several other instances in which white women falsely accused black men of rape. These men were killed, and later the white women recanted their stories and received no jail time or any type of punishment. Below are a couple of other instances where this happened:

1931 — Nine black boys from ages thirteen to nineteen were falsely accused in Alabama of raping two white women, Victoria Price and Ruby Bates, on a train near Scottsboro. Ruby Bates recanted her story. She was not charged. [106]

1955 — Carolyn Bryant accused Emmett Till of whistling and making sexual advances at her in the grocery store. He was brutally murdered at the age of fourteen for a lie. She admitted she lied in 2017. She was not charged.[107]

---

105 Merriam-Webster, s.v. "modus operandi(n.)," accessed July 5, 2020.

106 History.com Editors, "Scottsboro Boys," History, updated January 16.

107 Katie Reilly, "White Woman Whose Harassment Claim Led to Emmett Till's Lynching: 'That Part's Not True.'" TIME, January 27, 2017.

You will not find this in your history books because the authors only want to depict blacks as slaves or "the Boogie Man," so to speak, which is always in a demeaning manner. We have a rich history and culture, which is emulated quite often from lip injections, butt injections, dreadlocks, dance styles, and/or risking one's health to obtain the rich golden color of black people. I also keep saying to myself, the hatred of the black race must be deeper than skin color—but what?

Are those who hate us afraid of the obvious? *They* just might be the inferior one and that is why they try to intimidate with riots and mobs. Why do they do their crimes as a group? Because maybe, just maybe, if it were a one-on-one fight without weapons, they just might lose. Are those who lack self-esteem afraid that maybe, just maybe, if the playing field were equal, blacks would surpass them? Just something to think about. Or are they afraid that maybe, just maybe, we will do to them what they did to us? The thing about it is, we won't. We are not built that way. We just want an equal chance, that's all, to prove we are capable, just as qualified, to live out the same *American Dream*. Why is that so difficult?

Look at how strong the black race is, even throughout all of the injustices we encountered, and we are still here. We are resilient. When given an opportunity, we far exceed some whites. Here are some examples. Many years ago, all sports were dominated by whites only. Now look at the following sports: football, baseball, track, a superstar in golf, one in women's tennis and one on the rise. They are either all black, majority black, or at least an only black master of the sport—like Serena Williams. When given an equal opportunity, we excel.

We have even risen against all odds to having a bona fide African American man hold the highest office in the land—President! Ever since this happened, Congress did everything they could to undermine his presidency. Now, I ask this question: Why did they hate him; is it because he is black, a scholar, or both and they could not handle it?

WHAT IS REALLY IN THOSE HISTORY BOOKS?

We need to ensure we vote in our local election for the superintendent, get involved in parent-teacher conferences, and read our children's history books. Several textbook companies are allowing whitewashing to occur. See the examples below:

The Texas Education Agency purchased 138,930 copies of a book published by McGraw-Hill titled *World Geography*, referring to African slaves as "workers." What the hell! Sure, like they were getting paid. *Not!* I don't have to tell you slaves built this country, yet whites say we are lazy. Here is a caption from the book, and it should enrage you: "The Atlantic Slave Trade between the 1500s and 1800s brought millions of **workers** from Africa to the southern United States to work on agricultural plantations," the textbook caption reads. It appears on a page titled "Patterns of Immigration." Africans *did not* voluntarily hop on a slave ship to be trafficked, exploited, beaten, killed, raped, and separated to merely *work*. How insulting.[108]

---

108 Zoe Schlanger, "Company Apologizes for Texas Textbook Calling Slaves 'Workers': 'We Made a Mistake,'" Newsweek, October 4, 2015.

In a seventh-grade textbook titled *Virginia: History, Government, Geography*, chapter twenty-nine, titled "How the Negroes Lived under Slavery," depicted slaves as not all being unhappy slaves; they were servants from 1957 to the 1970s.[109] Let's play a role reversal. If whites were beaten into submission, would you consider them happy? I would venture to say, no! The first enslaved Africans were brought to Jamestown, Virginia, and the 1619 Project surely tells of the additional enslaved Africans brought to the beaches near Point Comfort, Hampton, Virginia, over four hundred years ago, mind you, against their will to work the lands of the white man for free. Now, there is talk of defunding any educational system teaching the 1619 Project! Why can't our truth be told?[110]

"Scholastic Pulls Children's Book Criticized for Depiction of Happy Slaves." This is yet another publisher who did not read the book for its content, which depicts slaves of former President George Washington as jovial workers. I have to applaud them for the following statement: "We believe that, without more historical background on the evils of slavery than this book for younger children can provide, the book may give a false impression of the reality of the lives of slaves and therefore should be withdrawn."[111] Of course, the book gives a false narrative of being a slave. Try looking at

---

109 Tanasia Kenney, "Mother Exposes Text in Texas History Book Suggesting Some Blacks Were Not 'Terribly Unhappy' with Being Enslaved," Atlanta Black Star, April 18, 2018.

110 Bradford Betz, "Trump Threatens to Defund Schools That Teach 1619 Project," Fox News, September 6, 2020.

111 Shamar Walters and Elisha Fieldstadt, "Scholastic Pulls Children's Book Criticized for Depiction of Happy Slaves," NBC News, January 18, 2016.

historical documentaries like *Twelve Years a Slave*, or let's go back to 1975 and 1976 and look at *Roots*. If that does not give a glimpse of life as a slave or a freed black man tossed back into slavery, then I don't know what will.

In Texas, another publishing company, Pearson, published *Prentice Hall Classics: A History of the United States*, which includes the following piece of erroneous history: "But the 'peculiar institution,' as Southerners came to call it, like all human institutions should not be oversimplified. While there were cruel masters who maimed or even killed their slaves (although killing and maiming were against the law in every state), there were also kind and generous owners. The institution was as complex as the people involved. Though most slaves were whipped at some point in their lives, a few never felt the lash. Nor did all slaves work in the fields. Some were house servants or skilled artisans. Many may not have even been terribly unhappy with their lot, for they knew no other."[112]

The aforementioned textbooks are reasons we need to vote at the local levels. First, when we have children, it requires us to get involved in their education. Yes, that means, *you* and *me*. We need to read the content of their textbooks. *We* are the first educators for our children. We are responsible for ensuring they know their history. Guess what, this means *you* and I need to invest in our children's learning. If we don't know it, guess what, *we* learn with them.

---

112 Annabelle Timsit and Annalisa Merelli, "For 10 Years, Students in Texas Have Used a History Text Book That Says Not All Slaves Were Unhappy," QUARTZ, May 11, 2018.

Please remember, God blessed us with children who come into this world free of hatred, for hatred is a learned behavior. Children are a blank slate—and the ages between birth to five years old are their formative years. They are little sponges. Start reading to them while they are in the womb. Once they are out, start teaching them.

It is our job, not the teacher's job, to ensure our children understand the homework and do the homework. Yes, it is time-consuming, but your children are your biggest most valuable investments. Aren't they worth it? Their education is worth more than buying everything they want or, most likely, did not earn or deserve. If we don't teach it to them, do you really want them to learn it in school where our history is distorted?

Being an active member in the educational system for our children prevents the continued whitewashing of our history. How can any of the authors and publishers allow this to go on? Did they actually sit down and have interviews with ancestors from that time frame? Did they sit down with any black historians to make sure this information was somewhat accurate? Most likely not. It was a way of uncomfortably interjecting something about the ugliness of this country's past, yet putting a Band-Aid on America's history to make it appear as if it were not as bad as it *appears*. News flash. Unfortunately, it is just that bad.

WHAT IF THIS HAPPENED TO WHITES
Let this sink in. Imagine being snatched like our ancestors from your native country, forced to board ships like animals,

chained to the belly of the ship (where other slaves died next to you), and brought to America. Once there, you are put on an auction block, naked, and examined like an animal to see if you are strong and fit to work the land or bear more children. Then forced to forget your native language, learn the language of the oppressor, but dared to *learn the oppressor's language*, because if you learned to read and write, you would be beaten or killed! Slaves lived in constant fear—so how was this not an evil act? What we don't need is our history whitewashed to cover the sins of their ancestors. *All* whites benefited from the free labor of slaves!

Although we may not have been taught this in high school, please know when Abraham Lincoln abolished slavery, it was not without a price. Some 979 slave owners were compensated three hundred dollars per slave to keep the local slave owners loyal to the Union. Remember, slaves were considered property. White men were compensated for ending slavery.[113] Then once slaves were freed, the white man didn't have anyone to work the land. Blacks were free, but free to do what? They owned nothing, had nothing, and guess what? They ended up back on the same plantations they were freed from, and Massa, again, was getting free labor after being paid per slave. The cycle continued.

WHAT IS OUR RESPONSIBILITY?

Now, what is required on our part? Our job is to know the superintendent of our county. Even if we do not have children

---

113 Jon Guttman, "Did Slave Owners Receive Compensation for the Loss of Slaves?," HISTORYNET, accessed June 1, 2020.

in school or never had children, we still need to know the name and platform of the superintendent. Even if we are empty nesters, we have an obligation to ensure the education of the children in our country is on the right side of history. If we cannot physically talk to any candidates, our vote is our way of talking to them. No, they will not know precisely who we are, but we know who we are and our responsibility. Not attending county school board meetings prevents us from knowing what is going on.

There may be a young mother in our neighborhood with little ones. Ask to see what they are learning in history class so we know if the information is right. Remember, it takes a village. Our village may be desegregated, but it takes a village none-theless. When *we* don't get involved in the voting process by learning the platform of each candidate at the local level, *we* are part of the problem.

If we desire not to vote or are in "our feelings" thinking our vote does not count, then *we* are disenfranchising our black communities, whether we live there or not. How are we helping the government disenfranchise black communities? Simple–not voting. As I asked earlier, if our vote were not important, why is our government working so hard to find many ways to block our votes?

If the Fifteenth Amendment granted blacks and all people born or naturalized as citizens in these United States, the right to vote, why is our government (the ones we either voted for or did not vote for) using so many tactics to prevent us from casting our vote? I will tell you why. *Black votes matter!*

In the past, during Reconstruction, blacks voted Republican and held office until the Union soldiers left and white Democrats regained power. That shifted in the 1960s, in which the majority of blacks voted Democrat because Democrats cared about people whereas Republicans began to only care about small government.

In summary, my recommendation is this. Study each candidate in all elections, even if this means making a table and putting their platform on it so you can evaluate each candidate side by side. Then, cast an educated and responsible vote for the candidate who aligns with your values and the concerns for black communities.

If you are a high school student who thinks your vote on this subject does not matter, this is where you are wrong. You, too, need to make sure what you are learning is right, and when you have children, what they are learning is right. It is not always about me and mine at the moment. You need to think about the black community and how your vote affects them.

We may be doing better than the next person, but we must always look back to see what we can do to help those who are less fortunate and how we can be of service.

* * *

QUESTION:

When you vote, will you consider the school system in the community where you live to ensure textbooks are on the right side of history or continue allowing authors and publishers to whitewash this country's past by putting a Band-Aid on it to make whites not *appear* as bad as it seemed?

CHAPTER 6

HEALTH CARE

———

If the Republicans fill this seat, the Supreme Court will be top-heavy with conservatives who want to get rid of the Affordable Care Act.

Health care is so vitally important today with COVID-19, and so are all the other health-care services everyone in America needs, such as basic annual checkups, dental, and vision. What about people who have preexisting diseases like diabetes, high blood pressure, mental health, fibromyalgia, and any other illnesses not mentioned? We are the ones most affected by COVID-19 due to our poor health.

If you are in high school or college, or have no children, you may think this topic does not affect you. On the contrary! Let's talk about how you are affected. Health care is very expensive today; shucks, it's always been. Affordable health care should be available to everyone. What does that have to do with you? Allow me to tell you. When I was growing up, thank God, we were healthy children with no broken bones and no major illnesses. The matriarch of the family, my mother, caring for five children and working at the post office, probably could not afford health care. Then again, I am not even sure how health care was paid for back then. If you were to get sick today, do you have any idea how much it costs to be transported by an ambulance? An ambulance's base rate and loading fees run between $600 and $2,100, depending on the services received while transported.[114]

DENTAL CARE

The first time I saw a dentist, that I can recall, was in the fifth grade. I lived with my Aunt Jean and Uncle Smitty, who was in the military and took me to the dentist; I had cavities! Man, the way the military dentists did a cavity, no matter how small, was to drill out the entire center of the tooth and replace it with mercury fillings. Remember, that was when I was in the fifth grade. Hmm, many moons later, I still have them, but now they need to be replaced because mercury leaks into the bloodstream, according to the dentists. Not a cheap process, and now I need crowns. Yes, crowns; but by God's grace, I can afford it today under the insurance plan with my employer.

Many parents don't discuss with children whether they can afford dental care. They teach you to brush your teeth. If they have dental care, then they take you to the dentist every six months for a checkup and your dentist teaches you about dental care. Umm, I don't recall going every six months—so when I say God watches out for babies and fools, He surely

---

114 Spend On Health, "How much does an ambulance cost?," accessed June 4, 2020.

covered me in this department. By His grace, I didn't even need braces and He knew my mother couldn't afford it.

AVERAGE BLACK CULTURE DIET

Blacks have a higher rate of diabetes and high blood pressure because of our diets. Our diets are culturally based, especially for those who hold strong to the culture because the food tastes so good. Of course, growing up, that is all we knew. There is nothing like a pot of beans with smoked ham hocks, pig feet, pig ears, chitterlings, smoked neck bones, and fried fat back. Whoa Lawd! Talk about some good eatin'.

Others are affected due to heredity, and no amount of exercise and eating healthy seems to cure it. As I got older and learned the benefits of foods I didn't like as a child growing up, like brussels sprouts and soggy asparagus from the can—yuck—I learned the health benefits and developed a taste for them. I also learned to get them fresh and season them well. My philosophy is: If it is healthy for me, then it becomes mind over matter—nasty versus healthy—uh, I'll take healthy, Alex, for two hundred dollars!

Here is one of the issues with trying to eat healthy—the cost. The cost to eat healthy comes at a price. It is not cheap; therefore, many of us cannot afford it, especially if we are living in poor communities. Let's look at the health-care system and its availability to all.

AFFORDABLE CARE ACT – DUBBED OBAMACARE

During President Obama's reign in office, his administration passed the Affordable Care Act, dubbed Obamacare by the Republicans because for one, it was supposed to be a negative connotation, and two, they were so dead set against it. Under this plan, people with preexisting illnesses are covered. This is vital because if someone had cancer, previously, insurance companies could deny coverage due to the illness or drop patients if they got too sick and/or became too costly to insure.[115]

President Obama understood this and thus, the Affordable Care Act was born. Under this act, people didn't have to make a lot of money or be in perfect health to be covered. If you chose not to purchase health care, under the individual mandate, the following year when you filed your taxes, you had to pay a fee for each month you were without health care, and you received documentation confirming or denying you were enrolled in a health care plan. I know this because I helped my son file his taxes. Personally, I liked this because everyone was paying into the health-care system. Before, people who were not covered still had to have their bill paid. Guess who ended up paying for their health care? When people could not pay, eventually, because of the increase in premiums, people who had health care paid the cost—you.[116]

Most countries have a universal health-care system in which everyone has health care. The Affordable Care Act is not

---

115   Obamacare USA, accessed July 27, 2020.

116   Maureen Groppe, "Who Pays When Someone Without Insurance Shows Up in the ER?" USA Today, July 13, 2017

perfect, but it was a start to something that could be perfected over time. I learned in my policy class that when policy is developed and implemented, it must be evaluated. That is when you assess what works and what doesn't work. You don't throw out the whole thing and start over. Simple, right? One would think. The Republicans' plan then and today is to gut the entire program without offering a solution. This will result in many Americans losing health-care coverage.

Since February 2020, the United States has been plagued with COVID-19. As of today, well over 210,000 are dead. Many blacks died disproportionately compared to other races due to our health issues like diabetes and high blood pressure. Perhaps this pandemic could have been put under some type of control early if there was a national plan. In my opinion, if we continue piecemealing how to tackle this virus, state by state, I foresee us never really getting this virus under control and we will be going through this for many years. The economy will take even longer to recover.

MEDICAID

Medicaid is a health-care program provided by the government (state and federal) for people needing financial assistance, such as low-income adults, children, pregnant women, elderly adults, and people with disabilities.[117] When medical professionals take Medicaid, they know this is a guaranteed payment. Surely most of you know someone who fits into this category, or you may be part of this category. The

---

117 Medicaid, Centers for Medicare and Medicaid Services, United States Government, accessed June 6, 2020.

Republicans want to cut Medicaid, meaning someone you know (such as grandparents), or even you, will lose health care. Still don't want to vote?

MEDICARE

This, too, is a health-care program provided by the government for people sixty-five and older, certain younger people with disabilities, and people who have end-stage renal disease. This is for people who are on dialysis or awaiting transplant due to permanent kidney failure.[118] Again, surely you know someone affected by this, or you may be affected. My brother was on Medicare when he contracted pneumonia with Legionnaires' disease, had a heart attack, and went into renal failure. He had just started a job two weeks prior but was not on the job long enough for their health insurance to cover him. Thank God for Medicare. He met one of the prerequisites: dialysis. Thank God, today, he is healthy.

While the Affordable Care Act, Medicaid, and Medicare provide health care to those who can and cannot afford health care, the best thing we can do is try to prevent the need for serious health care. We only get one life, one body, and when we're young, we think we are going to live forever. The lifestyle we live when we are young may result in one of the aforementioned health issues above. How can we take care of our bodies now? It is never too late to get our body in a healthier state. The key thing is we must eat healthier. Other than the people who have health issues due to heredity, think

---

118 Hello Medicare, "Medicare 101: How Medicare Works", Hello Medicare, accessed, June 6, 2020.

about other people we know with health issues. Ever wonder why? Much is due to diet and food deserts.

DIET

If our diet consists of fried foods constantly, lots of starches, sweets, pork, and a lot of meat with animal fat, these foods are surely going to cause health issues down the road. Trust me, I know these foods are tasty because I grew up on them. too, but we must eat a lot of green vegetables and lean meats. Starches like potatoes, beans, white rice, pasta, corn, white bread, and a lot of sweets like cakes and pies, to name a few, break down into sugar.

Have you ever wondered why you are so sleepy after a heavy meal full of the foods just mentioned? Too many carbs (starches) cause your blood sugar to spike quickly and then drop, resulting in a drop in blood sugar, called a sugar crash.[119] Over time, too many starches can cause diabetes. Let's take a typical Thanksgiving dinner. Have you ever thought about the number of calories in a Thanksgiving dinner? Here are the foods full of carbs, calories, and diabetes: cornbread dressing, macaroni and cheese, lima beans, yams or sweet potato soufflé, potato salad, sweet potato pie, and an assortment of cakes. This is most likely a two to three thousand calorie meal sure to put you to sleep! *We* are killing ourselves! This, we can control.

---

119 Karen Gardner, "Does Eating Carbs Make You Sleepy?" LIVESTRONG, August 16, 2019.

FOOD DESERTS

Food deserts are mainly in black inner-city neighborhoods and rural towns that don't have access to affordable, healthy, or fresh food because there is no grocery store. How can you determine if your neighborhood area is a food desert? Ask yourself these questions. Is the nearest grocery store greater than a mile from your home, and you don't have a car? Also, are there more convenience stores like 7-11, Circle K, Wawa, and Mini Marts where you live that do not have healthy choices? Is there a great variety of fast-food places near you that tend to serve fried foods or have fewer vegetables?[120]

The sad thing, too, is we frequent the fast-food place, and if they have vegetables, we either do not get them or select corn on the cob—which is a starch! If there is a vegetable, it might be fried—not good! One thing I know—Southern black folks will fry *err thang*! I recall visiting my husband's family in Murfreesboro, North Carolina, for a family gathering, and for the first time in my life, I ate a fried crab—or tried to eat it, and yes, it was good, too!

WE ARE OUR OWN WORST ENEMY

Now that you can identify where a food desert may be located, think about this: Why do you suppose there are food deserts in some places? During the recent riots after the murder of George Floyd all across the US, some protestors burned community businesses. These business owners invested their hard-earned money into their businesses and made

---

120 Ce'Dra Rogers, "The Food Desert Dilemma: 23+ Million Americans Lack Access to a Supermarket," Dr. Axe, May 13, 2018.

a choice to be in black neighborhoods to support the community. Now that the businesses are gone, innocent citizens who depended on the grocery store for healthy food or the pharmacy for medicine no longer have the support system to live comfortably. The result—a food desert.

You have to ask yourself this question: Why would that business owner rebuild in that neighborhood? That neighborhood is now a risky place to do business. There are major food deserts in inner cities due to high crime. Business owners are afraid of being robbed, which is unfortunate, because not only does this present a problem with getting fresh, affordable, and healthy food, but the community also loses job opportunities for citizens who are actually trying to do better or want better.

Let's not forget the children who will suffer from the food deserts. They need fresh food for proper development of the brain, as well as a great foundation for their health. Bad eating habits learned early in life continues throughout one's life, unless there is a health crisis that causes one to change eating habits. As we get older and realize this thing called our body is a gift from God, we will decide to eat healthy. We realize we are not going to live forever, and the aches and pains are a constant reminder we need to eat healthy, exercise, drink plenty of water, and expose the body to the sun daily for a few minutes.

SELF-CARE

You are probably wondering how we got on these topics when the chapter is about health care. Well, health care starts with self-care. If we don't start with caring for ourselves—our gift—we, too, can end up with serious health issues like some people we know (again, not those who have health issues due to heredity). This means not only do we need access to affordable fresh foods, but we also need to see a doctor, get checkups, and exercise. This is something many blacks in poor neighborhoods, and many educated and successful black men, will not do on a regular basis. Oftentimes, when they decide to go, it may be too late, but if an illness were detected earlier, the survival rate would be higher.

DISMANTLING OF AFFORDABLE CARE ACT – OBAMACARE

Affordable health care should be available to everyone. If this means we have to pay into it, so be it. This is why we need to vote in elections at the state level, because your congressional representatives (House of Representative and Senate) are the ones making decisions on our behalf regarding whether we will have health care, and if it will be one you can afford.

One thing the Republicans need to realize is dismantling the ACA to spite President Obama and the Democrats will end up hurting a lot of poor whites, too, who cannot afford health care either. The thing is when President Obama implemented the ACA, because of its complexity, the Republicans were having a difficult time getting rid of the whole thing, and without a replacement plan that incorporates some of the same things within President Obama's plan. Brilliant!

Are there areas that can be tweaked after being in existence? Yes. No plan is ever 100 percent great out the gate.

They should consider what is good and keep it. That which needs to be tweaked, tweak. Before it was about spending so much money, but the funding for COVID-19 helped put this country into a greater deficit. Without the ACA, many people would have to file bankruptcy.

Too many people relying on the ACA have preexisting diseases. If the plan the Republicans want to put in place will not cover them, they are going to be in trouble. After all, those with preexisting diseases need health care, too. To date, the ACA is still in effect; however, as I am editing this chapter, Justice Ruth Bader Ginsburg died four days ago, and the Senate is chomping at the bit to fill her seat before the election on November 3, 2020. If they fill this seat, the Supreme Court will be top-heavy with conservatives who want to get rid of the ACA, along with LGBTQ rights, Roe v. Wade, equal pay for women, and other issues.

The ACA is up for vote early November 2020, and there are only eight justices. Eight Supreme Court justices could yield a tie when voting on the ACA, as a few conservative justices voted against dismantling it. Confirming another conservative justice to replace Justice Ginsburg who wants to get rid of the current health-care system ensures a guaranteed dismantling of the ACA.

The death of Justice Ruth Bader Ginsburg revealed to the public what I already knew about the Senate. They make up new rules or change their minds when it benefits their agenda.

The Republicans prevented President Obama from selecting a justice. The excuse used was because it was an election year and the "people" should pick when they pick the president. Senators McConnell, Lindsay Graham, and all of the members are saying something different now that this is an election year.[121] They are rushing to confirm a conservative justice to ensure they have more conservatives, which not only has the possibility of dismantling the ACA but also other laws they feel are too liberal.

This is the third time the ACA will be looked at, and twice before, Chief Justice John Roberts cast the deciding vote upholding the ACA, stating the individual mandate was valid under Congress's taxing power. In 2017, the Republican-led Congress got rid of the individual mandate and dropped the tax penalty to zero. This is causing a big stir because now Texas and other Republican states feel that if there is no longer a tax penalty, then the individual mandate along with preexisting diseases should be unconstitutional, too, and thrown out.[122]

In summary, as you can see, the ACA has been a topic since President Obama put it in place. Initially, people were complaining and did not want to be forced to have health care. Now that they have it, they do not want it to stop. Currently, thirty-nine states (including DC) are participating in the Medicaid expansion with the federal government, "which

---

121 Amber Phillips, "Why Mitch McConnell Intends to Confirm a New Supreme Court Justice Now, When He Wouldn't in 2016," Washington Post, September 19, 2020.

122 Ariane de Vogue and Devan Cole, "Supreme Court Will Decide the Fate of the Affordable Care Act Sometime Next Term, Presumably after the Election," CNN, updated March 2, 2020.

is designed to provide low-income adults coverage options who could not afford health care or they had limited access to health coverage via their employer."[123]

States deciding not to participate resulted in their citizens paying taxes into a system they will not benefit from. See, the Medicaid expansion is fully funded through 2022 by the federal government and actually helps benefit a state's economy. "If all the states participated, over 21 million poor Americans will have access to basic health benefits by 2020."[124] If you ever heard people say their insurance increased significantly, it is because their state elected not to participate in the expansion. This decision is made at the Congressional level, and it's important to know how your representative feels about this topic.

Remember, it is not always about you, but about taking care of your fellow man, too. You may be able to afford health care, but you don't know if a person close to you is having a hard time and cannot afford it. If health care is important to you, your family, loved ones, and friends, this topic is too important to leave on the table without casting a vote.

Besides, you never know what is going to happen to you or your loved ones. States rejecting the expansion are Republican-led states. If you live in one of those states and, again,

---

123 KFF Organization, Status of State Medicaid Expansion Decisions, Interactive Map, October 1, 2020.

124 Ariane de Vogue and Devan Cole, "Supreme Court will decide the fate of the Affordable Care Act sometime next term, presumably after the election," CNN, updated March 2, 2020.

health care is important to you, then you know what you need to do. Remember, not voting means you, like the government, are disenfranchising your community, too.

* * *

QUESTIONS?

What illness needs to affect you or your family to make voting for health care a priority? COVID-19, diabetes, high blood pressure, cancer, autism, what?

CHAPTER 7

POLICE BRUTALITY & EXCESSIVE FORCE

———

"First time you violate that, you lose your license. . . . Now do you hate Niggers more than you like seeing your family? Then your behavior changes . . . you got to give them something they cannot afford to lose."

DICK GREGORY

There is no doubt, we are living during historical times where minority communities are demanding justice, not just in the United States, but across the world. It is as if God allowed COVID-19 to happen at this precise time because people are off work and able to go out and protest. Mr. George Floyd's death on May 25, 2020, culminated years of police shooting unarmed black men while running, while in front of their own home, or due to mistaken identity. Most recently, they have resorted to chokeholds or a knee to the carotid artery and throat, cutting off circulation and airways. Why did this killing upset the world? It was not until Mr. George

Floyd's killing was caught on camera, like others, but the world heard him pleading, "I can't breathe," over and over again, yet the police officer continued pressing his knee on his neck so cavalierly with his hand in his pocket, as if he were getting great pleasure from hearing a black man beg for his life and later call out to his dead mother! This is what tore the nation up so badly! Then, all hell broke loose!

Black, brown, white, and other races all over the world were protesting, not just for George Floyd, but for all minorities who died a senseless death. Now the world witnessed the brutality by our "finest" kill yet another black man when all of this could have easily been avoided. The world witnessed America, a country that has the audacity to police injustice in other parts of the world, ignore the cries of injustice on its soil. We live in a country where many white people thought racism was not an issue. Well, you know me; I have always thought to myself: "How can you think racism is no longer an issue?" In my opinion, it is for one or more of the following reasons:

- Some white people have little interactions with people of color in the workplace or after work.
- Some white people think since the country appears to be getting along, everything is good.
- Some white people think people of color are doing well, i.e., actors, actresses, and sports figures.
- Some white people don't look at the news to see what is happening around them.
- Some white people see the news but dismiss killings of people of color because the killings are not happening to their children; therefore, it does not impact their lives.

- Some white people think blacks deserve to die.
- Some white people just don't care.

Let me say this immediately. Not all white people fit in the aforementioned categories. There are so many white people who give more than a damn, who understand the plight of black people. There are many who open their homes to people of color, adopt them, feed the homeless, and donate their hard-earned money to causes affecting our communities, and then there are those who see us as the humans God created us to be. Many white people are implementing, or at least trying to implement, legislation that benefits us and all of America.

Many whites realize we have not been given a fair deal in "America" and took a chance on us, allowed us to compete, and hired us for jobs based on our merit—not the "good ole boy" system. Wait, as soon as I wrote that last statement, immediately I said, "You know doggone well blacks were never part of the 'good ole boy' system," and laughed, but many of you understand what I mean. There are whites who let their guard down to "get to know" others who don't look like them, realizing people who are different are not the enemy or evil—merely trying to have the "American Dream" and working hard as hell like the next person to have it. There are whites who are best friends with people of color and couldn't care less about skin color. This is very prevalent in the military.

The beauty of today is this current generation did not grow up in a segregated world. One of Dr. Martin Luther King, Jr.'s dreams in his famous speech at the Lincoln Memorial,

Washington, DC, was ". . . one day right there in Alabama little black boys and black girls will be able to join hands with little white boys and white girls as sisters and brothers."[125] Today, little black and brown boys and girls are joining hands with little white boys and girls because this was taught to them. As early as kindergarten, children simply play with one another because they want to play. Race is not a factor. As they go through grade school together, they've gotten to know one another.

Now, fifty-plus years later, from that iconic speech, little black and brown boys and girls are marrying little white boys and girls, producing another generation of biracial children who don't hate anyone based on the color of their skin. They grew up neither black nor white—often finding it hard to fit into either race. Guess what? They are people, we all are people. If we cut one another, we bleed the same red blood, just of a different blood type. If anyone is in need of a transplant, I guarantee you it will *not* be denied just because it came from a race of people you hate. You'll take it, and as a matter of fact, you won't even ask from whom it came before taking it.

So why do some whites just hate people of color? Here are some reasons I think this is so:

- Some whites do not want to mingle with people of color unless they are vacationing on islands where black people are waiting on them and treating them like royalty.
- Some whites still feel black people are not their equals, although we all came from a woman's womb.

____

125 Dr. Martin Luther King, Jr. Speech on Washington, August 28, 1963.

- Some whites feel black people should just be satisfied with what they have given us, ignorant to the fact that this world belongs to God; therefore, we and they own nothing. Everything any of us has can be wiped away in the blink of an eye. Besides, when you die, as Jimmy Hicks says, "I've never seen a Brinks truck backed up at a funeral."
- Some whites cannot handle the fact that no matter how much they try to oppress people of color, we don't bend. We still rise with resiliency.
- Some whites, as with the Black Wall Street, loathe the fact that people of color are becoming self-sufficient, acquiring things from their hard work, and perhaps are better off than them.
- Some whites feel slavery should have never ended; blacks will always be inferior to them, and deserve nothing.
- Then, you have some whites who hate us just because they are hateful people and this is what they are taught. When babies are born, they will love everyone until taught otherwise.

My point is that some of these very whites have infiltrated our police departments and are patrolling black communities. They share the same feelings about the people in our communities and have sniffed one another out. When on the streets, their focus is to see how they can get us for any little thing–either harassing us, locking us up, or eventually killing us. When they are seen killing a black man, why are there three or four attacking him at a time?

Let's look at cases in which some police officers used brutal excessive force, resulting in the deaths of unarmed blacks.

But first, let me say this. Regardless of the crime, if the officers' lives are *not* in any danger, especially when the suspect is in handcuffs or running away, the suspect should go to jail, face the crime, and be alive today. Too many police officers are trigger-happy or have this mentality that they are above the law. In most cases, they have been allowed to get away with murder.

MR. RODNEY KING

On March 3, 1991, the world watched in horror, for the first time, as four white Los Angeles, California, police officers were videoed beating Mr. King, an unarmed black man, like a wild animal. After a high-speed chase and arresting him for drunk driving, they were seen kicking and beating him with their clubs fifty-six times.[126] The four officers were charged with assault and excessive force but were later acquitted, even though the evidence was in everyone's face!

MR. AMADOU DIALLO

The killing of unarmed black people started long before Mr. George Floyd and recent others. Let's go back to February 4, 1999, when Mr. Amadou Diallo was killed outside his New York City apartment by police officers (Mr. Sean Carroll, Mr. Richard Murphy, Mr. Edward McMellon, and Mr. Kenneth Boss), who were in plain clothes, while he was attempting to enter his home. They mistook him for a rape suspect and fired a combined total of forty-one shots, of which nineteen

---

126 History.com Editors, "Rodney King Trial Verdict Announced," History, April 29, 1992.

struck him. While each officer was charged with second-degree murder and reckless endangerment, they were found not guilty and acquitted. The city settled and paid the family $3 million.[127]

MR. ERIC GARNER

On July 17, 2014, Mr. Eric Garner, an unarmed black man, was killed on the sidewalk of a local store on the suspicion of selling untaxed cigarettes. A New York City police officer, Daniel Pantaleo, put Garner in a prohibited chokehold during an arrest. Garner, forty-three, died shortly afterward. His last words were, "I can't breathe."[128] The "I Can't Breathe" movement resulted from this senseless killing. The grand jury found no reasonable cause to bring charges on the officer.[129] If the grand jury could not find a reason to charge the officer, why did the city settle out of court for $5.9 million?

MR. MICHAEL BROWN

On August 9, 2014, Michael Brown, an unarmed black man, was killed by police. Two witnesses state he was walking down the street with his friend, en route to his grandmother's house, when the police officer told him to "get the *f**k* on the

127 Rocco Paranscandola and Larry McShane, "NYPD Officer Acquitted in 41-Shot Killing of Unarmed Bronx Resident Amadou Diallo in 1999 Promoted to Sergeant," Daily News, December 17, 2015.

128 Christopher Mathias, "The Man Who Filmed the Eric Garner Video Is Behind Bars," HuffPost, October 5, 2016.

129 Associated Press, "From Eric Garner's Death to Firing of NYPD Officer: A Timeline of Key Events," USA Today, August 20, 2019.

sidewalk."[130] Of course, words were exchanged. So, I checked to see if walking down the street is a crime in Ferguson, and it is not. Why did his walking in the street incite such language? A video was released of Michael Brown robbing a convenience store, and I do not condone robbing of any kind. However, he was unarmed, and the robbery does not appear to be the reason for stopping Mr. Brown.

Witnesses said he had his hands raised, saying, "Don't shoot," but he was shot anyway–eight times. Officer Darren Wilson was not indicted for murder.[131] However, the city settled out of court with an undisclosed amount of money on a wrongful death lawsuit. If the actions of a police officer are justified and the jury finds them not guilty, why is the city paying money to the family under a wrongful death lawsuit?

MR. TAMIR RICE

On November 23, 2014, at the age of twelve, Tamir was shot by police because someone called 911, stating someone had a gun on the playground. The toy gun Tamir had looked like a real Colt M1911 because his friend removed the orange tip from the barrel while trying to fix it. The officer was not charged in his death.[132] The video shows Tamir playing alone in the snow. Ironically, the 911 caller told the dispatcher they did

---

130 Eliott C. McLaughlin, "What We Know about Michael Brown's Shooting," CNN, August 15, 2014.

131 Ibid.

132 The Guardian, "Tamir Rice: Police Release Video of 12-Year-Old's Shooting Fatal Shooting Video," November 26, 2014, YouTube 1:48.

not think the gun is real, but that message was never relayed to the officers. The city settled for $6 million.[133]

MR. WALTER SCOTT

On April 4, 2015, Mr. Walter Scott, an unarmed black man, was stopped for a nonfunctioning brake light, ran away from the scene, and was shot by a police officer, Michael Slager, in North Charleston, South Carolina. Officer Slager lied, stating Mr. Scott took his Taser and tried to use it on him, causing him to shoot Mr. Scott. Unbeknownst to the officer, a cell phone video posted online showed Mr. Scott running away from Officer Slager, who fired his weapon eight times. The video captures the most damaging footage of the officer tossing something from his belt near Mr. Scott's body. Officer Slager was indicted on a charge of murder and released on bond in January 2016. When he went to trial, he was not convicted because the case ended in a hung jury. Surely you are not surprised.[134] Eventually, he was convicted of deprivation of rights under color of law and obstruction of justice and sentenced to twenty years in prison, and the city settled a lawsuit for $6.5 million.[135]

133 Bob Adelmann, "Cleveland Settles Tamir Rice Shooting Lawsuit for $6 Million," The New American, April 26, 2016.

134 Matt Ford, "Shot and Killed While Running Away," The Atlantic, April 7, 2015

135 Alex Johnson, "South Carolina Town Settles with Walter Scott's Family for $6.5 Million," NBC News, October 8, 2015.

MR. FREDDIE CARLOS GRAY, JR.

On April 12, 2015, Mr. Gray, a twenty-five-year-old black man, was arrested for the possession of a switchblade in Baltimore, Maryland, which is considered a weapon.[136] I have been looking at the footage of his arrest but couldn't find anything indicating how they discovered Mr. Freddie Gray had a switchblade in the first place. "He was subsequently charged for possessing a knife." [137]

Subsequently means afterward, so the arrest came first. But why was he initially arrested? How did the police officers know he had a knife in the first place? The amount of force rendered to Mr. Gray was extreme and unnecessary, to the point this young man's spinal cord was severed.

It was obvious from all footage when the police officers were taking him to the back of the police transport van that he was in excruciating pain. He couldn't walk on his own, as his legs were dragging while the officers helped him to the van.[138] Then he endured a horrific ride to the police station due to the practice of not ensuring detainees were secured in the van and "giving them a rough ride to the police station." The six police officers (Caesar Goodson, Jr., William Porter, Edward Nero, Garrett Miller, Brian Rice, and Alicia White) who were charged with the death of Mr. Gray were

136 Tom Marlowe, "Maryland Knife Laws: What You Need to Know, Survival Sullivan," accessed July 29, 2020.

137 Joy-Ann Reid and Joy Y. Wang, "Police: Freddie Gray Arrested for Possession of Switchblade," MSNBC, April 30, 2015.

138 Suzanne Malveaux, "Video Shows Important Moment During Freddie Gray Arrest," CNN, April 22, 2015. YouTube,2:27.

acquitted and allowed to return to work. The city settled for
$6.4 million.[139]

MS. BREONNA TAYLOR

March 13, 2020, Ms. Breonna Taylor, a twenty-six-year-old
Louisville, Kentucky, EMT, was fatally shot while sleeping in
her bed by police officers as they barged into her apartment
under a "no-knock" order. Her boyfriend fired in self-de-
fense at the unknown intruders and shot one of the police
officers in the leg. Two other officers unloaded a barrage of
bullets into the apartment, killing Breonna. The boyfriend
was charged with shooting a police officer, but the grand
jury did not charge the police officers with Breonna Taylor's death. However, the grand jury did charge one officer,
Brett Hankison, with "first-degree wanton endangerment for
allegedly firing blindly into the apartment and endangering
neighbors."[140]

As you can expect, all hell broke loose again because another
black person was killed by police officers, except this time,
Breonna Taylor didn't see it coming. In September, the city
of Louisville settled for $12 million.

---

139 Ian Simpson, "Baltimore Offers $6.4 Million to Settle Freddie Gray Case,"
     Reuters, September 8, 2015.

140 Igor Derysh, "No Charges Filed Against Any of the Three Officers for
     the Killing of Breonna Taylor," Salon, September 23, 2020.

POLICE REFORM

I have been hearing recommendations to defund the police. It seems defunding them means releasing them from doing things they should be doing in the first place, such as doing welfare checks in homes or talking someone out of committing suicide. Why not invest money into mental health issues and the needs of each low-income community where the police seem to be in greater numbers? I would not ever recommend getting rid of the police department, because we need them. I do feel they need to be retrained on how to handle situations. Instead of being "on ready, set, shoot," how about trying to talk to the person like a human? Instead, after the fact, it's like, "Oops! I thought he was armed."

Dick Gregory made a profound and powerful recommendation about how to reform police officers. But if the idea is from a black man, what are the chances it will be put into law? Before I share exactly what he said about police reform, I'll preface it with a lesson we all know, as it relates to learning.

For example, once burned by a hot stove or oven, you will not touch it again because you *know* you will get burned. You know to look both ways before crossing the street because you might get hit by a car. You know if you do not study for an exam, for the most part, you will fail. You know if you do not pay your bills, services will be cut off. Each of these examples teach you to not touch a hot stove or oven, look both ways to avoid being hit by a car, study and prepare for an exam so you will pass it, and pay your bills on time to avoid services being cut off *and* credit score going in the toilet. You also know if you are caught driving without insurance, you will get a ticket and possibly lose your license until showing proof of insurance.

So, Dick Gregory had an excellent way police officers can learn to stop killing blacks without a cause. He said, "How do you make a cop change? Simple, you pass legislation and say every cop has to be insured. Everybody that carries a gun, got to be insured. First time you violate that, you lose your license. . . . Now, do you hate Niggers more than you like seeing your family? Then your behavior changes . . . you got to give them something they cannot afford to lose."[141]

That is a good darn recommendation to change the behavior of policemen. Like doctors and lawyers, you have to have insurance in case someone files a lawsuit against you, which ensures you are very careful when working with patients. Why not the same logic with police officers? This should make police officers very careful and actually *think* before pulling the trigger to kill a fleeing black man, doing a choke-hold, placing knees to the neck, or doing no-knock raids, which now have been outlawed. Who is more important—a black man or your family?

In summary, the names listed above could very well be the names of your family members and my family members—or even you or me. In each case, the police officers either used unnecessary excessive force during the apprehension of a suspect, or shot fleeing suspects in the back who, at the time of the flight, posed no threat to the officers. Police reform is at

---

141 Dick Gregory Interview, "How You Gonna Reform A Cop?" Reelblack, July 10, 2016, YouTube, 12:04.

the forefront of discussions today and long overdue since Mr. George Floyd's murder. The saving grace of years of police brutality, excessive force, and an officer's word against that of witnesses or the deceased is cell phone video footage. Videos do not lie!

This is why *you* need to be involved in elections at the local level, to ensure the mayors and police chiefs know what you want. If you have not been voting for these local elected officials—shame on you. If you are not participating in the process, then you do not have a leg to stand on when things go so terribly wrong. If you have not been voting in these local elections, you are not ensuring your community is safe. Everyone can deliver lip service, but lip service does not resolve issues, and you are part of the problem.

When your local officials do not hear from you, your issues never move past your thoughts and conversations. For example, as I write this book the Black Lives Matter Movement has been making their point loud and clear, but this will not solve the problem alone. You must vote in the local elections if you really want to be heard. It is unfortunate your elected officials call Black Lives Matter protestors everything but people who want change and are tired of the way blacks are treated.

This is how some elected officials feel about your pain as it relates to police brutality and excessive force. I will never condone burning a city and looting, but guess what, isn't this the very thing white mobs did to numerous black businesses, Black Wall Street, our ancestors' homes, and churches? As wrong as it is, it seems this is a behavior learned from the white mob when they show signs of hatred toward blacks. And they have been doing it for years, without consequences.

* * *

QUESTIONS?

What do you think police reform should look like? What can you do in your local community to ensure your opinion is heard?

CHAPTER 8

WHAT DO MY FRIENDS AND FAMILY KNOW AND THINK ABOUT VOTING

———

When you do not vote in these critical elections, it really doesn't matter who you put in office, because if your state's representatives do not align with the party of your presidential candidate, don't expect much to get done on your behalf.

During the process of writing this book, I thought it would be a good idea to poll my family and friends on their thought processes on voting. The sample was small in that the participants are people I know directly or indirectly via my then-fiancé Jimmy Hicks, who has been so supportive throughout this process.

Because voting is so near and dear to my heart, I am the one who ensures everyone is aware they need to vote. However, I was concerned about whether my friends knew the latest tactic by our government to suppress votes or disenfranchise voters—removing voters who have not voted in recent elections. Now you may say, *Well, this is across the board and not targeted at the black and brown race.* Not so fast. See, the state governments know who is voting and who is not voting. Guess who is not voting at a higher rate than white voters—you guessed it right—black and brown voters. Black and brown voters are not in tune to the voting process or who's running for office at the local and state levels, rarely vote every four years for the president, do not know the importance of their vote, or don't vote in general. Bingo, you are a candidate for removal from the voting registry. When you do find out, it's too late and you cannot vote. You find out when you attempt to vote in an upcoming election and are turned away because you have been removed from the registry. The only one to blame is *you.* We are responsible for exercising our right and always knowing our voting status.

To test the waters of how my family and friends think about voting, I developed a survey to find out how old they were when they first voted, who the candidates were, why they voted, if they felt their vote was valuable, issues important to them, whether they participated in elections at the local, state, and presidential levels, whether they voted for congressional seats, how they thought the government was going to recoup the trillions of dollars spent due to COVID-19, and the kicker: Were they aware states are removing people from the voter registry for not voting? I was shocked at some of the responses, especially from some of my very well-educated friends. Their responses made it clear to me this book is important, because if they did not know some things, or felt a certain way, how many others are in the same situation?

Please note, the responses to the survey are in no way meant to slander anyone. These are eye-opening results—and how will any of us know what we don't know until we are asked? What is most important is now they know. Again, the purpose of this book is to ensure everyone knows their rights and responsibility to vote and, prayerfully after knowing, will be hungry to get involved and stay connected with what is happening around them.

SURVEY RESULTS

Let's take a look at a few of the survey questions and responses:

1. The ages range from forty-seven to sixty-eight.
2. Educational level—from some college to PhD.
3. Are you aware you can be purged from the rolls for not voting? Eight yeses, nine noes, and one no response.
4. How old were you when you cast your first vote? The ages ranged from eighteen to fifty.
5. In what election did you cast your first vote? Ranged from Richard Nixon and John F. Kennedy to Barack Obama.
6. Why did you vote in that particular election:

- My grandfather was a slave, and we were always taught to register at eighteen to vote and *never* miss voting.
- It was the first time that I was eligible to vote and I wanted my voice to be heard.
- I had become old enough to vote and my dad made it clear that too many people had died for me to be able to vote.
- I felt it an honor and privilege to exercise my right to vote. I felt grown-up and I felt the spirit of our ancestors cheering me on!

- Because it was my right to vote and I felt that I should exercise my right to vote.
- After returning from overseas that particular year, I observed the inequalities that black individuals truly lacked under the US government as opposed to the country I had just returned home from.
- I was always cognizant that voting is about divvying up resources. I was aware that if I didn't or don't vote people into office who have my best interest and advocate for initiatives that support my daily livelihood, then I cannot expect tax dollars to be spent in my best interests. However, it wasn't until Senator Obama decided to run for president that I honestly believed that blacks could get an equal opportunity to obtain anything worthwhile in America. I was older when I first voted, and I realized the importance of speaking up and pushing for equality. Not to mention, as an African American, I couldn't afford not to vote (any longer). Also, it was long overdue for America to have a black man as president. I knew we were capable and knowledgeable enough to handle the task.
- Because I was old enough to vote and was following my dad's lead.
- I couldn't wait to be old enough to vote. That was the first year I was eligible to vote. I was taught by my parents and teachers.
- There was a female vice president on the ticket.
- I finally realized that my vote did count and I wanted to see some changes. I realized the sacrifice my ancestors and those before me made in order that I could have the right to vote.
- First, it was my right and obligation.
- It was time.

- I felt that finally my vote may make a difference and was fully engaged; whereas, previously, I was partially engaged—intellectually but not politically active. I rooted for the Democratic slate of candidates but was not motivated to vote. This was likely due to, but by no means an excuse, my mobile military lifestyle, first as a "brat" then as a military member and spouse. I have not missed an election, even if it was just for a dog catcher, I realize the importance of local elections in building a viable bench of candidates for state and national elections.
- I voted in state and local elections that year because I became of age and my parents always voted.
- An awakening from my parents on the importance of voting.
- Because I thought it was important to make my vote count.
- I was attending college and my immediate family, extended family, and college friends always strongly emphasized the importance of voting. After researching the presidential candidates for myself, I voted for the president that appeared to be more aligned with the issues and causes that were most important to me during the time I was in college.

IMPORTANT ISSUES

Regarding the question "What issues are important to you?" there was a mixture of responses for all the issues to follow: gun laws, immigration, environment/pollution/going green, equal pay for equal work, prison reform and the restoration of voting rights, increasing the minimum wage to fifteen dollars, health care, social security/retirement, and Medicare.

The write-in responses included the Voting Rights Act of 1965, education, women's rights, and judges on the Supreme Court (state and federal). Some included justice, equality, taxes, local elections, jobs/employment due to COVID-19, and voter suppression. Others included abortion, affordable care act, gerrymandering, voter ID, poll access, and registration access. Additional write-in issues were systematic purging of voter registration rolls, Roe v. Wade, support, advocacy, funding, health care of those with autism and other disabilities. Next, rehabilitation and inner-city support and help, civil rights and voting rules, and increased pay for school teachers were major concerns. Other issues included inequality of the judicial system when it comes to races and cultures outside of the Anglo-Saxon race, and prescription coverage for everyone so people will not have to carry that expense as they become older because it costs so much. Also, more mental health coverage is needed to help with the homeless. Justice system reform is greatly needed: equity in sentencing for crimes committed no matter your economic status (rich, middle-class, poor); race; ethnicity; religious affiliation; punishment should fit the crime; and no businesses running prisons and earning money in exchange for minorities doing cheap labor and keeping their businesses afloat. Senators, congressmen and women, and judges should have a ceiling for years and terms they serve and have no political affiliation. Some want balances in leadership—more ethnic representation for all citizens in Congress. Political system reforms: Congress does not determine their own raises; Congress cannot be voted for more than eight years; and candidates cannot get kickbacks or money from special interest groups when running for office.

As you can see, the issues important to them far exceed what I asked and are very valid concerns. In looking at the reasons why most of the group voted, you can determine the age category for most of them. Many first-time voters who stated they were told to register to vote—their grandfather was a slave and he said register to vote and never miss an election; it is my responsibility and my right; knowing what my ancestors went through so I could have the right—tend to be classified as baby boomers.

IMPORTANCE OF RESEARCH AND SANCTIFYING YOUR VOTE

One respondent, a forty-one-year-old member of Generation X, actually took the time to research the candidates to see which one aligned with their values and issues before casting a vote. Phenomenal work! Now that is not to say the rest did not do their homework, but only one mentioned that they did. Surprisingly, the two longest, in-depth responses were from those with PhDs, in that I assumed they were long-time voters as myself, yet they were very careful about their vote. They did not want to just give it away until they felt there was a candidate deserving of it. Both candidates voted for the first time when then-Senator Obama ran for president.

The question about knowing your state can purge you from the voter registry for not voting was a fifty-fifty response, only because one participant did not respond to the question. If this very small sampling shows approximately 50 percent of the participants were unaware they can be removed from the voting registry simply for not voting, how many more eligible black and brown voters do not have a clue? The answer, most likely, is the same amount, 50 percent, which could devastate election results if they do not know their status.

IS YOUR VOTE VALUABLE?

Another question from the survey was: Do you feel your vote is valuable? Why or why not? All but one responded yes. One responded, "I do now," which counts as a yes. One response was "maybe." Rationale: "I did until Russian interference, collusion with Russians, a niche competitor, all apparently later endorsed by the Republican senate. Mitch McConnell's refusal to introduce legislation to the floor that will protect our vote is even more disheartening. However, I know my vote is more important than ever. I will be fully engaged as a Biden campaign volunteer, just as I was for Obama, and at the polls as a volunteer, and, of course, by casting my vote."

VOTING IN CONGRESSIONAL ELECTIONS

When asked "Do you vote in elections for Senate or House seats?" the responses made me realize many blacks are fully educated about the role of Congress; however, there is still more education and awareness needed. If one person does not know the function of Congress, he is a weak link in the chain. There were a couple of responses in which either the participant did not know they could vote for them or the response was the participant just hadn't taken the time to vote. Both participants are about equal in stats and participated in approximately the same number of elections. I wonder if they truly have not voted for one of these seats because there is one in every presidential election. Again, I will make it my business to ensure everyone is fully aware of Congress, their distinct functions, the length of each term, and when the terms are up for election, and spread the word to their family and friends.

These results were very educational for me, as I hope they are for you. Many people are not aware of everything in the political process. At one time, I wanted no part of history or the voting process. It was not until I was studying at Georgetown that I was enlightened and became eager to learn more. For a while, life got in the way and the hunger dissipated; however, hearing voters were being purged from the voter registry in Georgia put that hunger back into me, and thus this book. I wanted to see if others were aware. Like me, they were not, so I sought to tell everyone in my circle. This really angered me because, once again, the states have come up with another creative way to ensure black people are not part of the voting process. I think what angered me most is the Supreme Court upholding this law. Of course, once the Supreme Court upholds one state, other states are getting on the bandwagon.

Here is why I have a problem with the Supreme Court which, by the way, consists of majority conservative judges because, I reiterate, the Republican Congress blocked Democrat President Obama from electing a justice to fill an empty seat. Remember, the Voting Rights Act of 1965 required states who had a history of creating and passing laws that suppressed black votes to get preclearance from the Supreme Court before implementing such a law. Recall again, in 2013, the Supreme Court, in a decision five-to-four, ruled section five was unconstitutional. "The Supreme Court ruled . . . that the coverage formula in section 4(b) of the VRA, which was used to determine the states and political subdivisions subject to section five pre-clearance, was unconstitutional."

I know this was mentioned in a previous chapter, but it is so important that it bears repeating to drive the point home. The Court did not invalidate the preclearance mechanism in the VRA per se; "it effectively halted its use by invalidating the formula that determined which places were subject to the preclearance obligation."[142] States no longer have to get preclearance, thus opening the doors for states to once again come up with the latest tactic, voter purge, to suppress votes.

WHEN POWER IS MORE IMPORTANT THAN "WE THE PEOPLE"

Again, I don't know how many times it has to be said, but every election is important. After Supreme Court Justice Scalia, who was highly conservative, died, the seat was left open for a more liberal justice nominated by the president; however, the Senate Republicans refused to hold any confirmation hearings for President Obama to fill the vacancy. As mentioned earlier, Mitch McConnell did everything he could, and successfully, I might add, to prevent President Obama from filling forty-six other judicial positions. This is the power of the Senate. They refused to hold confirmations because they felt the next president should be able to select the justice. Well, they wanted another conservative and were successful at that.

---

142 Chris Bondi, "5 Facts about the Voting Rights Act of 1965," NEWSMAX, November 2, 2015.

My, how the Republicans have changed their belief from four years ago. They are now flipping on their earlier decision to fill the seat of Justice Ruth Bader Ginsburg, twisting why they are rushing to fill the seat. This is another example of how the government twists the law to meet their agenda when they are in power.

If you don't know by now, please know this. Your state's representatives, known as your senators and congressmen/women, are the ones who ensure your presidential candidate is successful while in office. When you do not vote in these critical elections, it really doesn't matter who you put in office, because if congress does not align with the party of your presidential candidate, don't expect much to get done on your behalf.

In summary, it does not matter how old you are or your educational background, everyone's perspective on voting is different yet important. Many of us voted based on how we were taught to vote—passed down from one generation to another, and that is fine. The key thing is you are voting! Each of us has our own issues and personal views.

As we get older, our voting priorities change. What was important to me twenty years ago is not as important today. Twenty years ago, health care was not on my mind, but now it is. Years ago, the issue of pollution was not important, but COVID-19 and everyone staying home proved to me the earth is so polluted. Images on television showing Los Angeles seeing the skyline for the first time because there was no fog; fish appearing in waters that were polluted prior to COVID-19; and personally, experiencing spring from my office window in its entire duration with the cool breezes and nice days were as if Earth was saying, "Thank you! I can breathe."

If you are passionate about certain issues, I implore you to vote. Research the candidate who supports your issues and be sure to vote for the same party in the House and Senate elections. Otherwise, as with President Obama, your candidate's agenda will go nowhere. If your candidate cannot get his agenda passed because you did not pay attention at the polls, decided not to cast a vote for a congressional seat, or merely don't show up to vote, then you are now disenfranchising yourself and the issues important to you. If your issues are that important to you, ensure the right people are in place to make them happen. Whatever you do, do not select an unqualified person who you think will be your savior, for there is only one savior!

* * *

QUESTION?

Will you share these survey questions with your friends and family to understand their concerns? Will you teach them what they may not know?

CHAPTER 9

CALL TO ACTION –
YOUR RESPONSIBILITY

___

So, this is what we need when we go to vote: driver's license, voter registration card, a backpack with water and snacks, a portable cell phone charger, a small umbrella, and a small lawn chair or game chair—something to sit on in the event we are going to be in line for hours.

As I near the end of this book, this is the good stuff! This is the chapter where I challenge you to ensure you vote and tell you how to get there. I know many of you think your vote doesn't matter and will not change anything, and you are not alone. This book is written with you in mind. If you recall in the previous chapter, others felt their vote mattered, and these people were highly educated and well-rounded. However, not until the election of President Obama did they feel there was hope and their vote would make a difference.

When I created the questions for the survey, I started trying to remember, shoot, when did I cast my first vote? You know me, as I was told many years ago from a dear friend, Landis, "Google is your friend," so I attempted to see if my voting record was on the internet. I did not find my voting record from the early years, but it is listed as far back as they started capturing it electronically, and I have been voting in every election for quite some time. I may not have paid attention to what I was voting for back then, but one thing is for sure: Now I do my due diligence in researching candidates to see who is worthy of my vote. If their record does not align with mine, they do not get my vote. I take this thing called voting very seriously.

I want to make sure you are ready when you get to the polls to vote. I must ensure you are equipped with the knowledge to ensure you not only vote, but tell others to vote, and before voting, do your homework to research each candidate. Let's get started!

HOW TO REGISTER TO VOTE

At the age of eighteen, you are eligible to vote.

Visit USA.gov to learn the different ways to register to vote.

1. You can register in person at the Department of Motor Vehicles, or you may be able to register at an Armed Forces Recruitment Center. You must check the locations first, which you can find in the above link. If you see an organization holding a Voter Registration Drive, by all means, register there if you cannot get to the Department of Motor Vehicles.

2. You can register online at the link above. Here, you will learn how to register to vote and find the deadlines for voter registration in your state. You can download the National Mail Voter Registration Form. Simply fill it out online or print and complete by hand and mail it to the location listed for your state. There is also a video with a guide for new voters, along with a transcript for the hearing impaired. If you have questions, there is a toll-free number to call to have your questions answered.

3. If you are or know someone in the military or who lives overseas, know that the Federal Voting Assistance Program allows you to vote if the following conditions are met:

- US citizen living outside the US
- Service member stationed overseas
- Spouse or eligible family member of a service member stationed overseas. Register to vote and request an absentee ballot at fvap.gov.

CHECK YOUR VOTER REGISTRATION STATUS ONLINE OR RE-REGISTER

To check the status of your voter registration, visit Vote.org. It takes less than thirty seconds to enter your name, address, date of birth, email address, and cell phone number, and in less than a second, a screen pops up to let you know if you are registered.

When do you need to re-register to vote?

- If your name and address have not changed and you're an active voter, you should not have to re-register to vote or update your voter registration.
- If you've **moved permanently to another state**, visit USA. gov.
- If you move very close to the date of a presidential primary or general election, check with your old state. You may be able to vote by mail through your old state for that election.
- If you've moved **within your state** or changed your name, you need to update your voter registration with your new location or your new name.[143] Make sure you also update your state driver's license or state ID card before the election, if that's the voter ID you'll use.

NOW, DO YOUR HOMEWORK

Now you are registered to vote. The critical question is how do you go about selecting the best candidate? I've listed a couple of good websites to teach you how to do your homework on possible candidates.

Visit SmartVoter.org to learn how to judge each candidate. There are so many helpful tips to gather materials on each candidate, evaluate their stand on issues, find out about their leadership abilities, how others view this candidate, their campaign message, and so much more.

You also want to know how each candidate voted on issues. Visit AARP.org to find out the voting record of each candidate.

---

143 https://www.usa.gov/register-to-vote#item-214523

Once there, you will be informed to go to Congress.gov to get the voting records of the Congress members. Why is this important? First, knowledge is power! Just like you had to study for an exam in school, studying each candidate is just as important. Do your homework on the issues they state they support in commercials and on their brochures, but do not stop there. If they state they support issues that are of concern to you, find out how they are voting in Congress on these very issues. I say, "Put your vote where your mouth is." Also, find out how many times they were not present for a vote, and find out why they were not present. Just as when you don't vote, it is a vote for the other party, and it is the same here. When the candidate does not show up for the vote, it sends a signal that they support the issue, and it becomes a vote against that issue.

CASTING YOUR VOTE

You are registered, have checked your status to ensure your registration is current (no funny business), studied each candidate, researched their voting record in Congress, and know the location where you will cast your vote. Great job! Going to the polls to vote seems pretty simple, right? Well, if it were that simple, maybe there would be no need for this chapter. It's not that simple; although, it should very well be. Remember when I discussed closed polling places? If you have been paying attention to the news at all, you'll remember the June 9, 2020, primary. In counties in Atlanta, Georgia, where the population is predominantly African American, ironically, the voters were in line for hours and into the night because the polling place did not have enough booths, or the staff was new and did not know how to work the machines, etcetera.[144]

One problem or another always occurs when it comes to voting in counties heavily populated with African Americans. Why? They hope we will not stay. So, this is what we need when we go to vote: driver's license, voter registration card, a backpack with water and snacks, a portable cell phone charger, a small umbrella, and a small lawn chair or game chair—something to sit on in the event we are in line for hours, like Georgia for the primary where voters were in line for hours, hoping the problem would be fixed by the election. The reasons were a result of the White House administration tampering with the United States Postal Service, causing distrust about whether ballots would be counted, COVID-19, social distancing, and not to mention, citizens are ready for a change.

It is a shame we have to think this way, but if our vote is important enough for them to find ways to stop, block, or discourage us, we need to dig our heels in and prepare for the fight of our lives. Virginia and Georgia were not the only states; Florida experienced this in 2013 when Republicans discouraged over two hundred thousand voters.[145]

---

144 Kevin Collier, Cyrus Farivar, Dareh Gregorian and Ben Popken, "Georgia Election 'Catastrophe' in Largely Minority Areas Sparks Investigation," NBC News, update June 10, 2020.

145 Luke Johnson, "Florida Voting Lines Discourage 201,000 Voters Statewide: Report," HuffPost, January 24, 2013.

If knowing the Republican party is attempting to silence our voices, along with everything discussed in this book, does not motivate you to vote, perhaps hearing the voices of former slaves or sharecroppers will get your attention. Mind you, sharecropping was still taking place when I was four years old in the early 1960s. What was a sharecropper? Sharecroppers were freed slaves with nowhere to go but back to the plantation to work the land from whence they came and where former slave owners still treated them like they were slaves. The sad thing is, once again, our government did nothing to help freed slaves to own land.

After the Civil War, many thousands of freed slaves left the plantations for a better way of life. Well, if you have ever heard of the phrase "Forty Acres and a Mule," it came from General Sherman, a Union army general, who "issued a Special Field Order Number Fifteen, granting each freed family forty acres and a mule, temporarily on Georgia's coastal area and the islands."[146] His army, in an effort to help, even donated some of the mules that were not needed for the war. Back then, as it is now, land ownership was a big thing. Problem—recall that I stated the granting of the land was temporary? Right, because President Andrew Johnson ordered all the land to be returned to its previous owners if it were under federal control—as was the forty acres.

Here is where it gets worse. The government gave the freed slaves who owned the land, temporarily, an option. They could sign labor contracts with the planters, of course white

146 History.com Editors, Sharecropping, last updated June 7, 2019, accessed August 29, 2020.

planters, or be evicted off the land. Naturally, if you didn't own land, you were forced to work as laborers either on farms owned by whites or a plantation, thus the creation of the term sharecroppers. Former slaves, sharecroppers, rented small plots of land to work themselves and at the end of the year, they had to give part of their crops to the landowner.[147] By the way, please do not forget, the Thirteenth, Fourteenth, and Fifteenth Amendments were passed by this time. These sharecroppers were citizens who were supposed to have equal rights as the white man and were free to vote. Do you see something wrong with this picture? Again, the government did not do anything to help freed slaves and had no problem with them working the system as they did as slaves, free labor for the white man.

VOICES OF FORMER SLAVES

- Fannie Lou Hamer, Sharecropper[148]
- Part 1 – Hear Former Slaves Speak[149]
- Ex Slaves Talk about Slavery in the USA [150]
- This Woman Is Believed to be America's Last Slave [151]

---

147 Ibid.

148 Richard Johnson, Interview with Fannie Lou Hamer (1968). Posted May 19, 2017. YouTube, 2:32.

149 American Folklife Center, "Part 1 – Hear Former Slaves," posted November 23, 2009, YouTube, 10:00.

150 Brooks, John, "Ex Slaves Talk about Slavery in the USA," NBC News, 1999, posted October 11, 2016, YouTube: 9:54.

151 Amelia Boynton Robinson, "This Woman Is Believed to be America's Last Slave," April 9, 2019, YouTube, 3:58.

- Interview with Ex-Slave Aunt Harriet Smith – Part 1[152]
- Granny Interview (Slavery/Picking Cotton/Experiencing Heaven) [153]
- Ex-Slave and Oldest American Charlie Smith, Full Interview [154]
- Hear Rare Interviews with Former Slaves Recorded in the Early 1900s [155]
- The Actual Voices of Black Slaves Recorded Now Revealed [156]
- Voices From the Days of Slavery – Alice Gaston [157]
- Incidents in the Life of a Slave Girl – Part 1 [158]

BLACK WALL STREET INTERVIEW

- Black Wall Street Survivor – Eldoris *McCondichie*[159]

---

152 Sleeping Giant Wake Up, "Interview with Ex-Slave Aunt Harriet Smith – Part 1", November 26, 2017, YouTube, 3:58.

153 Eric Green, "Granny Interview (Slavery/Picking Cotton/Experiencing Heaven)," JClark Productions, April 16, 2014, Youtube, 28:42.

154 "Sleeping Giant Wake Up," Ex-Slave and Oldest American Charlie Smith Full Interview, September 28, 2017, YouTube, 29:18.

155 Tripp's Exposing the Matrix, "Hear Rare Interviews with Former Slaves Recorded in the Early 1900s," June 15, 2019, YouTube, 20:24.

156 The Intellectual Maroon, "The Actual Voices of Black Slaves Recorded Now Revealed," ABC News, Nightline, January 12, 1999, YouTube, 8:57.

157 Robert Sonkin, "Voices from the Days of Slavery – Alice Gaston, July 1941," Objet D'Art, May 10, 2015, YouTube:3:21.

158 Harriet Ann Jacobs, "Incidents in the Life of a Slave Girl – Part 1," Culain ruled by Venus, March 10, 2012, YouTube, 56:09.

159 Dik Rowland, "Black Wall Street Survivor – Eldoris *McCondichie*," posted September 21, 2010, YouTube, 14:35.

- Slavery by Another Name / Prologue / PBS [160]
- A Sharecropper's Voice [161]
- "The Rape of Recy Taylor: How Rosa Parks Helped a Sharecropper Report Her Assault & Seek Justice"[162]
- Barriers for Black Voters in the South in the Early 1960s / Iowans Return to Freedom Summer [163]
- Family of Sharecroppers Looks to the Future without Forgetting the Past[164]
- African Americans Recall 1960's Fight for Voting Rights[165]

If you took the time to view at least one of the videos and heard the voices of former slaves and sharecroppers in America, it is impossible for you to think you should sit on your vote. Listen to how one family pooled their resources together to purchase the very home they saw as they worked the fields. Do you still think your vote today is not important? The life of sharecroppers was either in your lifetime, your parents',

---

160 PBS, "Slavery by Another Name / Prologue / PBS," documentary, February 3, 2012, February 13, 2012, YouTube, 3:10.

161 Antoinette Harrell, "A Sharecropper's Voice," yourstory08, September 25, 2010, YouTube, 9:31.

162 Amy Goodwin and Juan Gonzales, "The Rape of Recy Taylor: How Rosa Parks Helped a Sharecropper Report Her Assault & Seek Justice," Democracy Now, December 20, 2017, YouTube, 18:27.

163 Iowa PBS, "Barriers for Black Voters in the South in the Early 1960s / Iowans Return to Freedom Summer," July 7, 2016, Youtube, 3:09.

164 Family of Sharecroppers Looks to the Future without Forgetting the Past, CBS, December 21, 2018, YouTube 3:04.

165 African Americans Recall 1960's Fight for Voting Rights, VOA News, March 4, 2015, YouTube, 3:49.

or grandparents' lifetime. In essence, it was not that long ago, which is so disturbing because we were freed! This chapter breaks my heart because the treatment of our people was worse than that of a dog. They treated dogs better than blacks. I watched each video and while I heard a few stories of how blacks were treated, actually hearing the voices of real slaves was gut-wrenching. This continues to encourage me to educate black and brown people on the importance of voting. If we don't know what happened before us, we will not know what is happening around or in front of us. If we don't appreciate the plight of black people from the not-so-recent past, we are doomed to repeat it.

Our duty is to be responsible citizens and exercise our constitutional right to vote under the Fifteenth Amendment. If you do not think your vote is important, you need to find a new purpose in life. I've stated before, voting is not just for you, but for those in your community and the county. There is a wealth of information on registering, re-registering if you moved or had a name change, researching the candidates, rechecking your voting status, and casting your vote for the best candidate you feel will represent your issues and make things happen. The only reason we are not living the life of a slave or sharecropper is that people knew the government was wrong and challenged the laws. Amazing. It is said that justice is blind, meaning cases were decided on the facts.

VOICES FROM FAMILY AND FRIENDS AND THE IMPORTANCE OF VOTING

The last two generations were very persistent about the importance of voting because every day they faced some type of injustice simply for being born black in America. They either witnessed injustice or knew someone who did, yet they refused to let this stop them from voting or dying to ensure their voices were heard for the same rights as the white man based on what is written in the US Constitution. If it were not for them, we would not be enjoying the freedoms of sitting anywhere on any public transportation, sitting in the same room with whites enjoying a meal, attending events, attending integrated public schools and universities, job opportunities, legislative opportunities, and most importantly, voting.

I interviewed several older people, intentionally, ranging from seventy to eighty-five, to get their perspective on voting since they grew up during the Civil Rights and Voting Rights era. What stuck out the most, not surprisingly, was the black movement of local leaders and pastors ensuring blacks not only registered, but voted. Their parents were either involved in civil rights or, if they could not vote, they made damn sure their children understood the importance of their vote. Even then, blacks knew this thing called voting was so powerful, the white man didn't want them to have it.

One of Fort Valley State University's beloved retired professors, Dr. Bellamy, Department Head of History, Geography, and Political Science, shared a few things about his experience through his daughter, Donnita Bellamy, about how he ensured students were registered to vote in local elections and, if need be, gave them rides to the polls. He also solicited other black-owned businesses in the community to help get students to the polls. His mother, perhaps like many during her time, could not read, but she was an example of instilling the importance of voting in Dr. Bellamy, which he not only instilled in his two daughters who, like him, are active participants in voting rights, but the students he impacted in the classroom and neighborhood.

Other Fort Valley graduates, Dean Palmer and Mrs. Palmer, worked with voter registration. The former Miss Fort Valley State College from 1956 to 1957, Mrs. Rounette Ragin Tabor, who considers me like a daughter, was taught the importance of voting, instilled this in her children, and continues exercising her right to vote today.

My Uncle Smitty, US Army Retired Command Sergeant Major and like a father to me, was reared in Kinston, North Carolina. He clearly understood the importance of voting because the military desegregated in 1948, a few years before he enlisted. He made sure to vote while serving, sometimes by absentee ballot, and continues voting today.

An enlightening interview with Mrs. Willa Lewis, reared in Petersburg, Virginia, and treats me as a daughter, is one of the wisest, most matter-of-fact women I know. I met her in 1986 while serving in the military at Fort McClellan, Alabama, in the Chemical Corps with her daughter and my dear friend, retired US Army Lieutenant Colonel Veronica Brown. She gave her perspective on the need for the Civil Rights Act of 1964 and the Voting Rights Act of 1965. Like the death of Mr. George Floyd was televised and outraged America, perhaps for the first time in America, the beatings of blacks on the Edmund Pettus Bridge in Selma, Alabama, exposed the hatred of blacks for trying to vote by none other than policemen, and must have turned the stomachs of whites because now the ugly truth was exposed. Something had to happen to save face. That statement is mine because we are still facing issues of civil and voting rights. She most definitely understood the importance of voting and continues voting today.

Other interviews with Mr. Willie Harris, US Army retired Master Sergeant, and Mr. Riley Williams, US Air Force retired Master Sergeant, spoke of interesting things. For instance, Mr. Harris recalled going with his father to cast his vote in the garage of the white man's home of the yard he cut and without incident. Imagine that, casting your vote in the garage of a white man's home! Mr. Williams revealed his grandparents, Mr. Riley Mason, born in 1890, and Mrs. Emma Gale Mason, born in 1895, voted in every election in New Orleans, Louisiana. As you can see, there was a time when blacks voted freely. Both men voted throughout their military careers, sometimes by absentee ballot, and continue voting today.

A striking interview of a dear friend who also lived in Louisiana, Mr. James Fletcher, US Army Retired Lieutenant Colonel and reared in Vacherie, hit me in my gut to hear and know someone who actually grew up on a plantation. He grew up on the Laurel Plantation located between New Orleans and Baton Rouge, sitting on the Mississippi River where slaves were imported.

Prior to the passage of the Voting Rights Act of 1965, black men could vote but had to pass a literacy test; therefore, they did not vote because they were too embarrassed to let people know they could not read or write their names.

Once the Civil Rights Act passed and black men knew they could vote, the white plantation owner offered to give free wine, whiskey, ham, or something in exchange for their vote. If he agreed, the owner ensured they got a ride to the polls and received their bribe the day before or the day of the election. As a young boy, James, the think tank, had a conversation with his father, Mr. Harold Fletcher, Sr., saying the owner will not know who you voted for so just vote for who you want. James learned that day if the owner's candidate did not win, his wrath would impact everyone on the plantation. That was a clear message that sticks with him today. He understood the sacrifices his father and other black men made to protect their families. Although they were free to vote, they were not voting freely. Can you imagine being told who to vote for and if their candidate lost, your family suffered?

Another interview by my cousin, Ms. Brenda M., reared in North Carolina, remembers as a little girl, when family members wanted to vote, they had to take something called a sugar vaccine before voting! They had two choices. Decide not to vote because they were not sure if the sugar vaccine was tainted and die, or they take the vaccine, put it under their tongue, but later spit it out to keep from dying.

Unfortunately, in the life of negroes, coloreds, blacks, and now African Americans, Lady Justice truly was and is blind. She was blind to the injustices of human beings and allowed the cruel treatment of blacks because white Southerners had a sense of entitlement—free labor at all costs. When we elect not to exercise our right to vote, we are letting down our families, neighbors, and those who came before us and put their lives on the line so we can live a better life than they did. If we do not hold this constitutional right sacred, history could very well repeat itself—if we don't use it, we will lose it.

* * *

QUESTION?

After seeing the videos of former slaves and sharecroppers, and reading the stories of people alive today, now do you see the significance of your vote?

ACKNOWLEDGMENTS

I would like to take this time to thank my family, friends, coworkers, and friends of friends, all of whom were very instrumental in ensuring my quest to educate minorities about the importance of voting became a reality. Without your support, this would not be possible. Thank you for believing in me, the topic, and its importance at this time in history.

I am humbled and grateful for support from Ginger Adams, April Barrett and Family, Paula Bedford and Family, Belisha Bessicks and Family, Michael Bouie and Family, Lanita Brevard, Joyce Brown, Kenneth Brown, Dr. Veronica Brown and Family, Emory W. Brownlee, Jr. and Family, André Burks and Family, Laverne Burks, Camille Butler and Family, Florence Cadogan and Family, Kimberly Clark and Family, Kristinn Watkins Coleman and Family, Glenn Cooper and Family, Charles Crawford and Family, Ferdinand Del Toro Beauchamp and Family, Monica DeWalt and Family, Kayla Dorsey, Kimberly Dorsey, Brittany Downing and Family, Bonnie Dunlap, André Fletcher and Family, Debra Fletcher and Family, Vickie Freeman and Family, Tarsha Freeman and Family, Pamela Garner and Family, Adam Gates and Family, Lynn Gillis, Lewis Graves and Family, John Graham and Family, Patrick Grimes and Family, Jerome Haggins and Family, Gloria Harrell, Jimmy Hicks, Ronald Hicks, Gregory Homer and Family, Bruce H. Huff, Sr., and Family, Allen Johnson, Narissia A. Johnson, Lynette Kee and Family, Susan G. Kelly-Bing and Family, Carole Kidd and Family, Burette A. King and Family, Kellie King-Walker and Family, Wanda King and Family, Nickey Knighton and Family, Eric Koester and Family, Larry Lawson and Family, Jenny Lindenbaum and Family, Bridget Love and Family, Pauline Mallard and Family, Shirley McCullough and Family, Lisa McKinnon, Cheryl McNeil-Jordan and Family, Rose E. McRae and Family, Robbie Plate Miles, Donald H. Miller and Family, Donald J. Miller, Dr. George R. Monk and Family, Lasonja Reed and Family, Regina Reese-Gilchrist, Richard Robinson and Family, Shirley D. Stephens, Diane Stewart, Alicia Swartz, Carolyn D. Tillery, Curtis Thompson and Family, Wanda Tonic and Family, Cynthia Tucker and Family, Alphonso Turner and Family, Dr. Wilfred Varlack, Fred Vinson and Family, Robert Walker, Jr., Christopher Ward, Steven J. Watson and Family, Felicia Webb, Landis Webb, Brad Weikel, Riley Williams and Family, and Kristin Young and Family.

There are many close supporters who I want to give an extra shout-out to for encouraging me to keep writing, who felt the topic was needed at this precise time in our history, and were frequent sounding boards: April Barrett, Lanita Brevard, Joyce Brown, Kenneth Brown, Dr. Veronica Brown, Florence Cadogan, Kristinn Watkins Coleman, Kimberly Dorsey, Debra Fletcher, Adam Gates, Shirley McCullough, Carolyn Tillery, Dr. Wilfred Varlack, Landis Webb, and Tracy Weldon.

I thank my Prayer Warriors, who were always there, praying for me this past year through many ups and downs, and sending loving words of encouragement: Paula Bedford, Kay Clark, Shelia Coleman, Lynette Kee, and Francene McCrae.

Lastly, I want to thank my incredible husband, Jimmy, who supported this effort 110 percent as I juggled numerous projects and may have been a bit unraveled. Not once did he complain, but instead pushed me to complete this labor of love by unselfishly giving me the space and time to write. He provided his gentle strength when I was weak, much love when I was exhausted, and has been the wind beneath my wings for eleven years. I love you ~

To each and every one of you, thank you for believing in me and this project, and for taking a chance on me, a first-time author. As we know, "It takes a village." Thank you for being my village. . . .

"JoJo"

APPENDIX

___

INTRODUCTION

ACLU. "Supreme Court Strikes Down Current Coverage Formula to Voting Rights Act." ACLU press release, June 25, 2013. Accessed April 25, 2020. https://www.aclu.org/press-releases/ supreme-court-strikes-down-current-coverage-formula-voting-rights-act-1.

Bondi, Chris. "The Voting Rights Act: What Is Preclearance?" *NEWSMAX*, November 9, 2015. https://www.newsmax.com/ FastFeatures/Voting-Rights-Act-preclearance/2015/11/09/ id/701375/.

Famighetti, Christopher. "Long Voting Lines: Explained." *Brennan Center for Justice*, November 4, 2016. https://www.brennancenter.org/our-work/research-reports/long-voting-lines-explained.

Harvey, Josephine. "Trump Threatens To Yank Funding From Schools That Teach 1619 Project." *HuffPost*, September 6, 2020.

https://www.huffpost.com/entry/trump-1619-project-funding_n_5f556a47c5b62b3add4270fd.

Kessler, Glenn. "When Did Mitch McConnell Say He Wanted to Make Obama a One-Term President?" *Washington Post,* January 11, 2017. https://www.washingtonpost.com/news/fact-checker/wp/2017/01/11/when-did-mitch-mcconnell-say-he-wanted-to-make-obama-a-one-term-president/.

Madison, Joe. SiriusXM, *Urban View.* Channel 126. Accessed 2015.

National Constitution Center. "14th and 15th Amendments." Accessed April 3, 2020. https://www.constitutioncenter.org/interactive-constitution/amendment/amendment-xiv.

The United States Department of Justice. "Section 4 of the Voting Rights Act." Accessed September 12, 2020. https://www.justice.gov/crt/section-4-voting-rights-act.

Urban Dictionary Online. s.v. "Self-Disenfranchisement." Accessed March 12, 2020. https://www.urbandictionary.com/define.php?term=Self%20Disenfranchisement.

Whitaker, Morgan. "Virginia Republicans Celebrate Inauguration with Gerrymandering." *MSNBC News,* January 22, 2013. http://www.msnbc.com/politicsnation/virginia-republicans-celebrate-inauguration-w.

CHAPTER 1

American Historama. "The Reconstruction Act." Updated January 9, 2018. Accessed April 4, 2020. http://www.

american-historama.org/1866-1881-reconstruction-era/reconstruction-acts-1867.htm.

Bing. s.v. "Direct Disenfranchisement." Accessed April 3, 2020. https://www.bing.com/search?q=direct+disenfranchisement&cvid=a4bf859b85c947f7ab73eb10ef3f9c96&pglt=43&FORM=ANNTA1&PC=U531.

Bing. s.v. "Indirect Disenfranchisement." Accessed April 3, 2020. https://www.bing.com/search?q=direct+disenfranchisement&cvid=a4bf859b85c947f7ab73eb10ef3f9c96&pglt=43&FORM=ANNTA1&PC=U531.

Constitutional Law Reporter. "Harper v. Virginia Board of Election - Poll Tax Law Violated Equal Protection Clause." Accessed April 5, 2020. https://constitutionallawreporter.com/2018/11/02/harper-v-virginia-board-of-elections-poll-tax-violated-equal-protection-clause%ef%bb%bf/.

Cornell Law School. Legal Information Institute. "United States v. Reese Et Al." Accessed April 14, 2020. https://www.law.cornell.edu/supremecourt/text/92/214.

Forner, Eric. *Reconstruction: America's Unfinished Revolution*. Quoted in Debo Adegbile, "The Killing of Jimmy Lee Jackson." *The Marshall Project*, February 27, 2015. https://www.themarshallproject.org/2015/02/27/the-killing-of-jimmie-lee-jackson.

Foner, Eric. *Reconstruction: America's Unfinished Revolution*, 1989, 531. Quoted in J. Morgan Kousser, *The Shaping of Southern Politics: Suffrage Restriction and the Establishment of the One-Party South, 1880-1910*, Yale University Press, 1974, and Samuel

Issacharoff, Pamela Karlan, and Richard Pildes, *The Law of Democracy*, University of Michigan: Foundation Press, 1998.

Jervis, Rick. "Black Americans Got the Right to Vote 150 Years Ago, but Voter Suppression Still a Problem." *USA Today*, February 3, 2020. https://www.usatoday.com/story/news/nation/2020/02/03/black-voting-rights-15th-amendment-still-challenged-after-150-years/4587160002/.

JRank Articles. "White Primary – Party, Court, African, and Americans." Accessed April 10, 2020. https://law.jrank.org/pages/11301/White-Primary.html#ixzz6alx5Wito.

JUSTIA US Supreme Court. "Breedlove v. Suttles, 302 U.S. 277 (1937)." Accessed September 14, 2020. https://supreme.justia.com/cases/federal/us/302/277/.

JUSTIA US Supreme Court. "United States v. Cruikshank, 92 U.S. 542 (1875)." Page 92 U.S. 548. https://supreme.justia.com/cases/federal/us/92/542/.

Kousser, J. Morgan. *The Shaping of Southern Politics*. Quoted in "Techniques of Direct Disenfranchisement." *University of Michigan*, 26. Accessed April 9, 2020.

Kousser, J. Morgan. "The Shaping of Southern Politics: Suffrage Restriction and the Establishment of the One-Party South, 1880-1910." *Yale Historical Publications*: Miscellany Series.

Levine, Terry. "Sincere Ignorance and Conscientious Stupidity." Quote by Dr. Martin Luther King, Jr. *Noggin*, July 11,

2011. https://www.terrylevine.com/2011/07/sincere-igno-rance-and-conscientious-stupidity.html.

National Archives. "19th Amendment Ratified June 4, 1919, Passed August 18, 1920." Accessed April 4, 2020. https://www.archives.gov/founding-docs/amendments-11-27.

Onion, Rebecca. "Take the Impossible 'Literacy' Test Louisiana Gave Black Voters in the 1960s." *SLATE*, June 28, 2013. https://slate.com/human-interest/2013/06/voting-rights-and-the-su-preme-court-the-impossible-literacy-test-louisiana-used-to-give-black-voters.html.

University of Michigan. "Techniques of Direct Disenfranchise-ment." Accessed April 9, 2020. http://www.umich.edu/~law-race/disenfranchise1.htm.

University of Michigan. "Techniques of Direct Disenfran-chisement." Quoted in Eric Foner, *Reconstruction*, 1989, 531. Accessed September 14, 2020. http://www.umich.edu/~lawrace/disenfranchise1.htm.

University of Michigan. "Techniques of Direct Disenfranchise-ment." Quoted from J. Morgan Kousser. *The Shaping of South-ern Politics: Suffrage Restriction and the Establishment of the One-Party South, 1880-1910*. Yale University Press, 1974; and Samuel Issacharoff, Pamela Karlan and Richard Pildes, *The Law of Democracy*. Foundation Press, 1998. 263. http://www.umich.edu/~lawrace/disenfranchise1.htm.

"A Brief History of African American Voter Disenfranchisement." *US Slave* (blog). June 23, 2013. https://usslave.blogspot.com/2013/06/a-brief-history-of-African American.html.

CHAPTER 2

Bing. s.v. "Direct Disenfranchisement." Accessed April 9, 2020. https://www.bing.com/search?q=direct+disenfranchisement&cvid=a4bf859b85c947f7ab73eb10ef3f9c96&pglt=43&-FORM=ANNTA1&PC=U531.

Bing. s.v. "Indirect Disenfranchisement." Accessed April 9, 2020. https://www.bing.com/search?q=direct+disenfranchisement&cvid=a4bf859b85c947f7ab73eb10ef3f9c96&pglt=43&-FORM=ANNTA1&PC=U531.

Bureau of Prisons. Statistics: Inmate Race. Accessed September 16, 2020. https://www.bop.gov/about/statistics/statistics_inmate_race.jsp.

Oliver, John. "Voting by Mail." *Last Week Tonight with John Oliver.* HBO, May 31, 2020. YouTube, 19:11. https://www.youtube.com/watch?v=l-nEHkgm_Gk&t=86s.

Department of Homeland Security. "Real ID." Accessed April 19, 2020. https://www.dhs.gov/real-id.

Gramlich, John. "Federal Prison Population Fell during Obama's Term, Reversing Recent Trend." *Pew Research Center.* January 5, 2017. https://www.pewresearch.org/fact-tank/2017/01/05/federal-prison-population-fell-during-obamas-term-reversing-recent-trend/#:~:text=Federal%20prison%20population%20

fell%20during%20Obama%E2%80%99s%20term%2C%20
reversing,of%20data%20from%20the%20Bureau%20of%20
Justice%20Statistics.

Holtz, Michael. "Redistricting or gerrymandering? N.C. dispute embodies national debate." Science Christian Monitor, March 11, 2016. https://www.csmonitor.com/USA/Politics/2016/0311/Redistricting-or-gerrymandering-N.C.-dispute-embodies-national-debate.

JRank Articles. "White Primary – Party, Court, African, and Americans." Accessed April 10, 2020. https://law.jrank.org/pages/11301/White-Primary.html#ixzz6alx5Wito.

Kessler, Glenn. "When did Mitch McConnell Say He Wanted to Make Obama a One-Term President?" *The Washington Post*, January 11, 2017. https://www.washingtonpost.com/news/fact-checker/wp/2017/01/11/when-did-mitch-mcconnell-say-he-wanted-to-make-obama-a-one-term-president/.

Kousser, J. Morgan. *The Shaping of Southern Politics: Suffrage Restriction and the Establishment of the One-Party South, 1880-1910.* Yale University Press, 1974; and Samuel Issacharoff, Pamela Karlan and Richard Pildes, *The Law of Democracy.* University of Michigan: Foundation Press, 1998. Quoted in Techniques of Direct Disenfranchisement. *University of Michigan.* http://www.umich.edu/~lawrace/disenfranchise1.htm.

Lapin, Tamar. "Chris Christie Says It Was 'Serious Failure' Not to Wear Mask at White House." *The New York Post*, September 21, 2020. https://nypost.com/2020/10/21/chris-christie-i-paid-for-it-for-not-wearing-mask-at-white-house/.

Lemieux, Scott. "Equal Representation Won a Qualified Victory at the Supreme Court." *New Republic*, April 4, 2016. https://newrepublic.com/article/132370/equal-representation-won-qualified-victory-supreme-court.

Murse, Tom. "Where People Convicted of Felonies Can Vote in the U.S." *ThoughtCo*, Updated September 12, 2020. https://www.thoughtco.com/where-felons-can-and-cannot-vote-3367689.

Rouan, Rick and Doug Caruso. "Ohio's Voter Registration Purge Targeted Thousands in Error. Now, a Call for Change." *The Columbus Dispatch and USA TODAY Network*. Updated January 24, 2020. www.usatoday.com/in-depth/news/investigation/2020/01/22errors-ohio-voter-registration-purge-prompt-call-change/4490821002/.

State of Wisconsin Department of Transportation, Department of Motor Vehicles. Accessed April 21, 2020. https://wisconsindot.gov/Pages/dmv/license-drvs/how-to-apply/id-card.aspx.

Sullivan, Andy. "Southern U.S. States Have Closed 1,200 Polling Places in Recent Years: Rights Group." Reuters, September 10, 2019. https://www.reuters.com/article/us-usa-election-locations-idUSKCN1VVo 9J.

Techniques of Direct Disenfranchisement, 1880-1965. http://www.umich.edu/~lawrace/disenfranchise1.htm.

The DMV.ORG. "The DMV Made Simple." Accessed September 16, 2020. www.dmv.org/required.

Vasilogambros, Matt. "Polling Places in Black Communities Continue to Close Ahead of November Elections." *GOVERNING*, September 5, 2018. https://www.governing.com/topics/politics/sl-polling-place-close-ahead-of-november-elections-black-voters.html.

Wilson, Reid. "States Purge Millions of Voters: Report." *THE HILL*, August 1, 2019. https://thehill.com/homenews/campaign/455815-states-purge-millions-of-voters-report.

Wong, Kathleen. "This Wisconsin Man Brought 3 Forms of Identification to the Polls and Still Couldn't Vote." *Yahoo News*, April 14, 2016. https://news.yahoo.com/wisconsin-man-brought-3-forms-145500057.html.

CHAPTER 3

Empak Enterprises. "A Salute to Black . . ." *Black History Publication Series*. Vols. I, III, and IX, 1989.

Bellis, Mary. "10 Important Black Inventors in U.S. History." *ThoughtCO*, updated January 25, 2019. https://www.thoughtco.com/black-inventors-through-the-years-4145354.

The Editors of Encyclopaedia Britannica. "The Voting Rights Act." *Britannica,* updated July 20, 2020. https://www.britannica.com/event/Voting-Rights-Act.

Collins Dictionary. s.v. "servitude (n.)." Accessed April 20, 2020. https://www.collinsdictionary.com/dictionary/english/servitude.

Cornell Law School. "Plessy v. Ferguson." *Supreme Court*. Accessed September 20, 2020. https://www.law.cornell.edu/supreme-court/text/163/537.

GovInfo. "The Civil Rights Act of 1964." Accessed September 20, 2020. https://www.govinfo.gov/features/civil-rights-act.

Jaide, Don. "Plessy v. Ferguson: The Meaning of the 'One-Drop' Rule." *Africare Source*, November 20, 2011. https://www.afri-caresource.com/rasta/sesostris-the-great-the-egyptian-hercu-les/plessy-vs-ferguson-the-meaning-of-one-drop-rule/.

Johnson, Kevin Rashid. "Opinion U.S. Prison, Prison Labor Is Modern Slavery. I've Been Sent to Solitary for Speaking Out." *The Guardian*, August 23, 2018. https://www.theguardian.com/commentisfree/2018/aug/23/prisoner-speak-out-american-slave-labor-strike.

Lopez, Amy. "Texas Voting Chief Who Led Botched Voter Purge Resigns." National Public Radio. WAMU 88.5, May 28, 2019. https://www.npr.org/2019/05/28/727528998/texas-voting-chief-who-led-botched-voter-purge-resigns.

National Archives. "The Constitution of the United States." Accessed April 20, 2020. https://www.archives.gov/found-ing-docs/constitution_7492902.

Quigley, Bill. "40 Reasons Why Our Jails Are Full of Black and Poor People." *HuffPost*, June 2, 2015. https://www.huffpost.com/entry/40-reasons-why-our-jails-are-full-of-black-and-poor-people_b_7492902.

Vox, Lisa. "The Civil Rights Act of 1964 Did Not End the Movement For Equality." *ThoughtCo,* Updated February 14, 2019. https://www.thoughtco.com/the-civil-rights-act-of-1964-45353.

Williams, Pete. "Supreme Court Gives Ohio Right to Purge Thousands of Voters from Its Rolls." *NBC News,* June 11, 2018. https://www.nbcnews.com/politics/supreme-court/ohio-wins-supreme-court-fight-over-voter-registration-n873226.

CHAPTER 4

Bible Hub. "Matthew 18:22." https://biblehub.com/matthew/18-22.htm.

Blake, Matthew. "42 Facticate. Powerful Facts about Ruth Bader Ginsburg." *Factinate.* Accessed 3 October 2020. https://www.factinate.com/people/ruth-bader-ginsburg-facts/.

Congressional Votes Database. "Voting Records." *Govtracks.* Accessed September 22, 2020. https://www.govtrack.us/congress/votes.

Davis. Susan. "Senate Republicans Agree to Block Obama's Supreme Court Nominee." *NPR,* February 23, 2016. https://www.npr.org/2016/02/23/467860960/senate-republicans-agree-to-block-obamas-supreme-court-nominee#:~:text=Senate%20Republicans%20Agree%20To%20Block%20Obama%27s%20Supreme%20Court,Republicans%20Agree%20To%20Block%20Obama%27s%20Supreme%20Court%20Nominee.

History.com Editors. "Electoral College." *History,* Updated September 27, 2019. https://www.history.com/topics/us-presidents/electoral-college.

Langevin, Jim. "Understanding Congress." Accessed March 28, 2020. https://langevin.house.gov/about-me/understanding-congress#members.

Mataconis, Doug. "Virginia Governor Restores Voting Rights to 200,000 Ex-Felons." *Outside the Beltway,* April 23, 2016. https://www.outsidethebeltway.com/virginia-governor-restores-voting-rights-to-200000-ex-felons/.

National League of Cities. "City Council." Accessed September 20, 2020. https://www.nlc.org/city-councils.

Prince William County Government. "Virginia Government E-documents." Accessed August 4, 2020. https://eservice.pwcgov.org/documents/bocs/briefs/2020/0428/res20-330.pdf.

Schoolhouse Rock. "I'm Just a Bill," YouTube, 3:00. https://www.youtube.com/watch?v=tyeJ5503Elo.

U.S. Debt Clock. Accessed October 18, 2020. https://usdebtclock.org/.

Wesley, Reverend Dr. Howard John. "Birth of a Nation, Part 2." Alfred Street Baptist Church, Alexandria, Virginia. July 14, 2020. YouTube, 44.41. https://www.youtube.com/watch?v=9Topfx4OMM4.

CHAPTER 5

Betz, Bradford. "Trump Threatens to Defund Schools That Teach 1619 Project." *Fox News*, September 6, 2020. https://www.fox5dc.com/news/trump-threatens-to-defund-schools-that-teach-1619-project.

Cambridge Dictionary. s.v. "whitewashing (n.)." Accessed September 23, 2020. https://dictionary.cambridge.org/us/dictionary/english/whitewashing.

Clark, Alexis. "Tulsa's 'Black Wall Street' Flourished as a Self-Contained Hub in Early 1900s." *History*, updated January 2, 2020. https://www.history.com/news/black-wall-street-tulsa-race-massacre.

Dieff, Kevin. "An African Country Reckons with Its History of Selling Slaves." *Washington Post*, January 29, 2018. https://www.washingtonpost.com/world/africa/an-african-country-reckons-with-its-history-of-selling-slaves/2018/01/29/5234f5aa-ff9a-11e7-86b9-8908743c79dd_story.html.

Gates, Henry Lewis, Jr. "What Is Juneteenth." Originally posted on *The Root* (blog). PBS, *African Americans, Many Rivers to Cross*. Accessed June 25, 2020. https://www.pbs.org/wnet/African Americans-many-rivers-to-cross/history/what-is-juneteenth/.

Guttman, John. "Did Slave Owners Receive Compensation for the Loss of Slaves?" *HISTORYNET*. Accessed June 1, 2020. https://www.historynet.com/did-slave-owners-receive-compensation-for-the-loss-of-slaves.htm.

History.com Editors. "Scottsboro Boys." *History,* Updated January 16, 2020. https://www.history.com/topics/great-depression/scottsboro-boys.

Kenney, Tanasia. "Mother Exposes Text in Texas History Book Suggesting Some Blacks Were Not 'Terribly Unhappy' with Being Enslaved." *Atlanta Black Star,* April 18, 2018. https://atlantablackstar.com/2018/04/18/mother-exposes-text-texas-history-book-suggesting-blacks-not-terribly-unhappy-enslaved/.

Merriam-Webster. s.v. "modus operandi (n.)." Accessed September 24, 2020. https://www.merriam-webster.com/dictionary/modus%20operandi.

National Constitution Center. "13th Amendment. Abolition of Slavery." *Interactive Constitution.* Accessed May 16, 2020. https://constitutioncenter.org/interactive-constitution/amendment/amendment-xiii.

Reilly, Katie. "White Woman Whose Harassment Claim Led to Emmett Till's Lynching: 'That Part's Not True.'" *TIME,* January 27, 2017. https://time.com/4652126/emmett-till-carolyn-bryant-donham/.

Schlanger, Zoe. "Company Apologizes for Texas Textbook Calling Slaves 'Workers': 'We Made a Mistake.'" *Newsweek,* October 4, 2015. https://www.newsweek.com/company-behind-texas-textbook-calling-slaves-workers-apologizes-we-made-380168.

Walters, Shamar and Elisha Fieldstadt. "Scholastic Pulls Children's Book Criticized for Depiction of Happy Slaves." *NBC News,*

January 18, 2016. https://www.nbcnews.com/news/us-news/
scholastic-pulls-children-s-book-criticized-depiction-hap-
py-slaves-n498986.

Sullivan, Ken. "Throwback Thursday: Mississippi & the Thirteenth
Amendment 2013." *Cosmic Observation*, updated February 16,
2020. https://cosmic-observation.com/tag/ken-sullivan/.

Tang, Terry. "Juneteenth Marks Days Last Enslaved People Free."
AP Explains. AP News, June 18, 2020. https://apnews.com/arti-
cle/b8ce1d6f0e8b0e7269a8c569ffd52389.

The Constitution of the United States. "Bill of Rights and All
Amendments, 13th Amendment." Accessed June 12, 2020.
https://constitutionus.com/#n11.

Timsit, Annabelle & Annalisa Merelli. "For 10 Years, Students
in Texas Have Used a History Text Book That Says Not All
Slaves Were Unhappy." *QUARTZ*, May 11, 2018. https://
qz.com/1273998/for-10-years-students-from-texas-have-been-
using-a-history-textbook-that-says-not-all-slaves-were-un-
happy/.

CHAPTER 6

Centers for Medicare and Medicaid Services. "Medicaid." *United
States Government.* Accessed June 6, 2020. https://www.med-
icaid.gov/medicaid/index.html.

de Vogue, Ariane and Devan Cole. "Supreme Court Will Decide
the Fate of the Affordable Care Act Sometime Next Term,
Presumably after the Election." *CNN*, Updated March 2, 2020.

https://www.cnn.com/2020/03/02/politics/supreme-court-affordable-care-act-case-next-term/index.html.

Gardner, Karen. "Does Eating Carbs Make You Sleepy?" *LIVESTRONG*, August 16, 2019.

https://www.livestrong.com/article/530662-does-eating-carbs-make-you-sleepy/.

Groppe, Maureen. "Who Pays When Someone without Insurance Shows up in the ER?" *USA Today*, July 13, 2017. https://www.usatoday.com/story/news/politics/2017/07/03/who-pays-when-someone-without-insurance-shows-up-er/445756001/.

Hello Medicare. "Medicare 101: how Medicare Works." Accessed June 6, 2020. https://www.bing.com/search?q=define+medicare&cvid=3a664c1f69dd4bbfbd8e0d5ba0ce0141&FORM=ANNTA1&PC=U531.

KFF Organization. "Status of State Medicaid Expansion Decisions, Interactive Map." October 1, 2020. https://www.kff.org/medicaid/issue-brief/status-of-state-medicaid-expansion-decisions-interactive-map/.

Obamacare USA. Accessed July 27, 2020. https://www.obamacareusa.org/?;2CPCN_bi3uGVxJDQtzP75DTIXZlo-RMJLjncPoTj1_6urCUTVvxbCnKAgVXC_TG89rxsyL-Bhi&msclkid=521587db00c21c48d0a7d934cef2ff19.

Phillips, Amber. "Why Mitch Mcconnell Intends to Confirm a New Supreme Court Justice Now, When He Wouldn't in 2016." *Washington Post*, September 19, 2020. https://www.msn.com/

en-us/news/politics/why-mitch-mcconnell-intends-to-confirm-a-new-supreme-court-justice-now-when-he-wouldn-e2-80-99t-in-2016/ar-BB19c6HH.

Rogers, Ce'Dra. "The Food Desert Dilemma: 23+ Million Americans Lack Access to a Supermarket." *Dr. Axe,* May 13, 2018. https://draxe.com/health/food-desert/.

Spend on Health. "How Much Does an Ambulance Cost?" Accessed June 4, 2020. https://spendonhealth.com/ambulance-cost/.

CHAPTER 7

Adelmann, Bob. "Cleveland Settles Tamir Rice Shooting Lawsuit for $6 Million." *The New American*, April 26, 2016. https:// thenewamerican.com/cleveland-settles-tamir-rice-shooting-lawsuit-for-6-million/.

Associated Press. "From Eric Garner's Death to Firing of NYPD Officer: A Timeline of Key Events." *USA Today,* August 20, 2019. https://www.usatoday.com/story/news/2019/08/20/eric-garner-timeline-chokehold-death-daniel-pantaleo-fired/2059708001/.

Derysh, Igor, "No Charges Filed against Any of the Three Officers for the Killing of Breonna Taylor." *Salon,* September 23, 2020. https://www.salon.com/2020/09/23/one-police-officer-indicted-on-wanton-endangerment-charges-in-breonna-taylor-death-investigation/.

Ford, Matt. "Shot and Killed While Running Away." *The Atlantic,* April 7, 2015. https://www.theatlantic.com/politics/archive/2015/04/shot-and-killed-while-running-away/389976/.

History.com Editors. "Rodney King Trial Verdict Announced." *History*, April 29, 1992. https://www.history.com/this-day-in-history/rodney-king-trial-verdict-announced.

Johnson, Alex. "South Carolina Town Settles with Walter Scott's Family for $6.5 Million." *NBC News,* October 8, 2015. https://www.nbcnews.com/storyline/walter-scott-shooting/south-carolina-town-settles-walter-scotts-family-6-5-million-n441426.

King, Dr. Martin Luther, Jr. "Speech on Washington." August 28, 1963.

McLaughlin, Eliott C. "What We Know about Michael Brown's shooting." *CNN*, August 15, 2014. https://www.cnn.com/2014/08/11/us/missouri-ferguson-michael-brown-what-we-know/index.html.

Malveaux, Suzanne. "Video Shows Important Moment during Freddie Gray Arrest." *CNN*, April 22, 2015. YouTube,2:27. https://www.youtube.com/watch?v=xXMTPGf3fFM.

Marlowe, Tom. "Maryland Knife Laws: What You Need to Know." *Survival Sullivan*." Accessed July 29, 2020. https://www.survivalsullivan.com/maryland-knife-laws/.

Mathias, Christopher. "The Man Who Filmed the Eric Garner Video Is Behind Bars." *HuffPost*, October 5, 2016. https://www.huffpost.com/entry/ramsey-orta-eric-garner_n_57f5019ae4b-04c71d6f12ba4.

Paranscandola, Rocco and Larry McShane. "NYPD Officer Acquitted in 41-Shot Killing of Unarmed Bronx Resident Amadou

Diallo in 1999 Promoted to Sergeant." *Daily News*, December 17, 2015. https://www.nydailynews.com/new-york/nypd-involved-amadou-diallo-slay-promoted-sergeant-article-1.

Reelback. Dick Gregory Interview, "How You Gonna Reform A Cop?" July 10, 2016, YouTube, 12:04. https://www.youtube.com/watch?v=dRrAajModnU.

Reid, Joy-Ann and Joy Y. Wang, "Police: Freddie Gray Arrested for Possession of Switchblade." *MSNBC*, April 30, 2015. https://www.msnbc.com/msnbc/baltimore-protest-police-report-msna585481.

Simpson, Ian. "Baltimore Offers $6.4 million to Settle Freddie Gray Case." Reuters, September 8, 2015. https://www.reuters.com/article/us-usa-police-baltimore-idUSKCN0R81TZ20150908.

The Guardian. "Tamir Rice: Police Release Video of 12-Year-Old's Shooting Fatal Shooting Video." November 26, 2014, YouTube. 1:48. https://www.theguardian.com/us-news/video/2014/nov/26/cleveland-video-tamir-rice-shooting-police.

CHAPTER 8

Bondi, Chris. "5 Facts about the Voting Rights Act of 1965." *NEWSMAX*, November 2, 2015. https://www.newsmax.com/FastFeatures/voting-rights-1965-act-facts/2015/11/02/id/700208/.

CHAPTER 9

AL.com. "This Woman Is Believed to be America's Last Slave." Uploaded April 19, 2019. YouTube, 3:58. https://www.youtube.com/watch?v=Piq4JO8HVmk.

Brooks, John. "Ex Slaves Talk about Slavery in the USA." Posted October 11, 2016. YouTube, 9:54. https://www.youtube.com/watch?v=fZfcc21c6Uo.

"Family of Sharecroppers Looks to the Future without Forgetting the Past." *CBS*. December 21, 2018. YouTube, 3:04. https://www.youtube.com/watch?v=FV2IoO3hHjU.

Collier, Kevin, Cyrus Farivar, Dareh Gregorian, and Ben Popken. "Georgia Election 'Catastrophe' in Largely Minority Areas Sparks Investigation." *NBC News*. Updated June 10, 2020. https://www.nbcnews.com/politics/2020-election/georgia-secretary-state-launches-investigation-after-unacceptable-voting-problems-n1228541.

Green, Eric. "Granny Interview (Slavery/Picking Cotton/Experiencing Heaven)." *JClark Productions*. April 16, 2014. YouTube, 28:42. https://www.youtube.com/watch?v=MFJHhrFgRYg.

Goodwin, Amy and Juan Gonzales. "The Rape of Recy Taylor: How Rosa Parks Helped a Sharecropper Report Her Assault & Seek Justice." *Democracy Now*. December 20, 2017. YouTube, 18:27. https://www.youtube.com/watch?v=6BJgNUrS38c.

Harrell, Antoinette. "A Sharecropper's Voice." *yourstory08*, September 25, 2010. YouTube, 9:31. https://www.youtube.com/watch?v=6wNi4h8TEF4.

History.com Editors. "Sharecropping." *History.* Last updated June 7, 2019. https://www.history.com/topics/black-history/sharecropping.

Iowa PBS. "Barriers for black Voters in the South in the Early 1960 / Iowans Return to Freedom Summer." Posted July 7, 2016. YouTube, 3:09. https://www.youtube.com/watch?v=aOM6xnh4ddc.

Jacobs, Harriet Ann. "Incidents in the Life of a Slave Girl – Part 1." *Culain ruled by Venus*, March 10, 2012. YouTube, 56:09. https://www.youtube.com/watch?v=04Ktmxg2QgY.

Johnson, Luke. "Florida Voting Lines Discourage 201,000 Voters Statewide: Report." *HuffPost*, January 24, 2013. https://www.huffpost.com/entry/florida-voting-lines-report_n_2544373.

Johnson, Richard. "Interview with Fannie Lou Hamer (1968)." Posted May 19, 2017. YouTube, 2:32. https://www.youtube.com/watch?v=Nhu_uxRR2og.

PBS. "Slavery by Another Name / Prologue / PBS," documentary, February 3, 2012. Aired February 13, 2012. YouTube, 3:10. https://www.youtube.com/watch?v=DjUF1ktxxIQ.

Rowland, Dik. "Black Wall Street Survivor; Eldoris McCondichie." Posted September 21, 2010. YouTube, 14:35. https://www.youtube.com/watch?v=lx62joRN-YU.

Sleeping Giant Wake Up. "Ex-Slave And Oldest American Charlie Smith Full Interview." September 28, 2017. YouTube, 29:18. https://www.youtube.com/watch?v=MXYzu_kNx-Q.

Sleeping Giant Wake Up. "Interview with Ex-Slave Aunt Harriet Smith – Part 1." Posted November26, 2017. YouTube, 3:58. https://www.youtube.com/watch?v=Yy4xm8DtUu.

Sonkin, Robert. "Voices From the Days of Slavery – Alice Gaston, July 1941." *Objet D'Art*, May 10, 2015. YouTube, 3:21. https://www.youtube.com/watch?v=9UqY3sxHIyE.

Tripp's Exposing The Matrix. "Hear Rare Interviews with Former Slaves Recorded in the Early 1900s." June 15, 2019. YouTube, 20:24. https://www.youtube.com/watch?v=6xDOlSbOIjg.

The Intellectual Maroon. "The Actual Voices of Black Slaves Recorded Now Revealed." ABC News, *Nightline*. January 12, 1999. YouTube, 8:57. ttps://www.youtube.com/watch?v=SZnUi2cH7yg.

Thesecretstorm. "Part 1 Hear Former Slaves Speak." Uploaded November 23, 2007. YouTube, 10:00. https://www.youtube.com/watch?v=3VTFkyDrH3M.

VOA News. "African Americans Recall 1960's Fight for Voting Rights." Posted March 4, 2015. YouTube, 3:49. https://www.youtube.com/watch?v=XywskQgBagk.

* * *

VOTER REGISTRATION LINKS:

How to Register to Vote - www.usa.gov/register-to-vote

Absentee Voting or Voting by Mail - https://www.usa.gov/absentee-voting#item-37337

Check Your Voter Registration Status - www.vote.org/am-i-registered-to-vote

Register to Vote - https://www.usa.gov/register-to-vote#item-212645

How to Judge a Candidate - http://www.smartvoter.org/voter/judgecan.html.

Six Ways to Check Out a Candidate - https://www.aarp.org/politics-society/government-elections/info-2018/politicians-answer-background-guide.html.